the bottom

a theopoetic of the streets

the bottom

a theopoetic of the streets

charles lattimore howard

CHANGEMAKERS
BOOKS

Winchester, UK
Washington, USA

JOHN HUNT PUBLISHING

First published by Changemakers Books, 2020
Changemakers Books is an imprint of John Hunt Publishing Ltd., No. 3 East Street,
Alresford, Hampshire SO24 9EE, UK
office@jhpbooks.com
www.johnhuntpublishing.com
www.changemakers-books.com

For distributor details and how to order please visit the 'Ordering' section on our website.

Text copyright: Charles Lattimore Howard 2019

ISBN: 978 1 78904 508 6
978 1 78904 509 3 (ebook)
Library of Congress Control Number: 2019952239

Scripture quotations marked NIV are taken from the Holy Bible, New International Version®,
NIV® Copyright ©1973, 1978, 1984, 2011 by Biblica, Inc.® Used by permission. All rights
reserved worldwide

A CIP catalogue record for this book is available from the British Library.

Design: Stuart Davies

UK: Printed and bound by CPI Group (UK) Ltd, Croydon, CR0 4YY
US: Printed and bound by Thomson-Shore, 7300 West Joy Road, Dexter, MI 48130

We operate a distinctive and ethical publishing philosophy in
all areas of our business, from our global network of authors to
production and worldwide distribution.

Contents

acknowledgements   1

preface   4

the bottom: a theopoetic of the streets   9

postlude   173

about the author   180

note from the author   181

endnotes   182

Also by Charles Lattimore Howard

The Souls of Poor Folk (edited) ISBN-13: 978-0761838562
The Awe and The Awful ISBN-13: 978-1482763843
Black Theology as Mass Movement ISBN-13: 978-1349476299
Pond River Ocean Rain ISBN-13: 978-1501831034

*The foxes have holes
and the birds of the air have nests
but the Son of Man
hath nowhere to lay his head.*[1]

acknowledgements

Loved. There hasn't been a day in my life when I didn't know that I was loved.

I won't endeavor to name all who have taken up residence in my heart, yet I will name a few of the places and institutions that my heart has called home—and it is to the following that I dedicate this book.

Since I first ran on the track at Franklin Field as a wide-eyed sophomore in high school, the University of Pennsylvania has been my home. As student, alum, hospital chaplain, associate chaplain, and finally as university chaplain, I have continued to grow and learn in this wonderful community. I will forever remain grateful that you took a risk on me when I first applied, and you have continued to believe in me all these years. *Leges sine moribus vanae.*

The first Latin motto that I was to learn, however, was *In tuo lumine lumen.* For twelve years, much of my formation occurred at the Gilman School in Baltimore, Maryland. My teachers, coaches and classmates there were and are my family. I graduated feeling prepared for whatever path awaited me. Thank you.

Each summer after school, let out from the ages of twelve through twenty-one, I would fly up to Boston and then take a bus the remainder of the way to Naples, Maine and spend June, July and August with "the best bunch of guys around." Basketball, football, soccer, swimming, all sports, all day, all summer was a dream come true. And I got to do it with kids who became some of my most cherished friends. The dad in me is also thankful for the chance to serve as a counselor there while in college. The way that you all "welcomed the stranger among you" is something that I often remember in my vocational work. *Todah Rabah.*

Just days after my final college course, I moved up to a town just outside of Boston and began my studies at Andover

Newton Theological School (now Andover Newton Seminary). I cherished my three years there. Between sitting under the brilliance of my professors, worshiping in chapel, or working in the campus bookstore reading books in between sales, I learned just what ministry is. I would choose Andover Newton again and again.

Ben Valentin and Kirk Jones, my advisers at Andover Newton, encouraged me to pursue doctoral work after seminary. I was reluctant as I feared "climbing too high away from the streets" (something that inspired this book, I now realize). I'm grateful that they saw something in me that I could not see in myself. I ended up being accepted into the PhD program at Lutheran Theological Seminary of Philadelphia (now United Lutheran Seminary). What a faithful and encouraging intellectual and spiritual community they are there! I'm very proud to have your name on my diploma and your colors on my academic hood.

My church homes over the years—Rose of Sharon, New Psalmist, Ruggles, Common Cathedral, Trinity Copley, Church of the Good Samaritan, Narberth Pres, and the Philadelphia Episcopal Cathedral—have all loved me, loved my family, and drawn me closer to our God.

It is to all of the institutions above—academic, recreational, and ecclesial—that I dedicate this book.

And while the dedication is extended to these institutions, I must articulate special gratitude to the following:

Tim Ward and the team at Changemakers Books who believed in this project and put up with my haggling about the title. Thank you, Tim.

To the first readers who encouraged me through some very real insecurity to finish this project: Dana Richie Troy, Mary LeCates, Kirk Byron Jones, Jane Hart, and Ruth Naomi Floyd.

My siblings, Chucky, Joey, Yvonne, Stef, Ami, Trinah, Moe, Coey, Petey, Sarah, Curtis, Rich, and Steve. I love having you as my sisters and brothers—some by birth, some by marriage, some by choice, all by love.

John and Christine. I am sure Charlie and Audrey thank you—as do I—for the way you've stepped into my life.

And finally, to my utterly inspiring daughters, Charissa Faith, Annalise Hope, and Evangeline Love. You are "beyond category." I love you so very much.

I was about to put this project down. But then my wife, Dr. Lia C. Howard, read it in one sitting. She turned to me and said, "You have to publish this."

The strength and courage to keep going has so often come from my beloved. You have made life so much more fun, and you have made me a better scholar, better minister, better father, and better human. I love you and am so glad that you are my better third.

preface

Baltimore in the 1970s and 1980s, like the Baltimore of Freddie Gray, demanded that young Black men be brave. Every day. And I learned that courage fighting on the streets of the mid-Atlantic port town where I was born and raised.

It was under the weeping willow tree that stood somberly in front of my apartment building that I had my first street fight. I wasn't alone. At my side were battle-tested warriors who came to help me fight off these bad guys who had invaded our neighborhood.

Today, I find myself frustrated when individuals are characterized as "bad guys" or as "evil." Humans are complex and we all have a story. We all have a reason for doing what we do.

But these were legit bad guys.

Villains who came to my 'hood with one mission. The total destruction of our planet.

I sprung out my door and dove behind the tree that served as our base of operations. What the invaders did not know was that I had the power of flight. That—along with my invisibility, kinetic energy blasts, and power to read minds—made me a formidable foe for any adversary intent on doing us harm.

I sent my boy T'Challa to move in first and get some recon on the enemy. Storm created a cloud cover for us. Cyborg hacked into their computer systems to slow them down.[2] Finally, I would move in and rescue my mom from the evil alien Klansman trying to enslave Black folks again. And just as I stood face to face with their powerful grand wizard I heard from the front door of my building: "Poopee! Dinner!"

My mom's voice calls me back to our dinner table and back to reality.

It was when fighting racist super-villain aliens that I

first learned courage. Or to be more specific, it was in my imagination that I first learned courage. More than thirty years later, I recognize the irony in my retreating to the worlds that I created in my mind. These imaginary courageous journeys were a survival tactic—a mental escape from the real battles my eight-year-old self was too scared to engage.

My mom was dying. My father had just lost his job due to racism in his field. And it was all way too much for me. From age eight through my mother's death when I was eleven and even well into my teen years when my father would also pass, I used the one real superpower that I had—my imagination. When the reality of my life became unbearable I easily jumped to a world where it was safer—where the pain and grief of loss and racism could be escaped. Or maybe in my imagination, I had the courage and the tools to work for healing and to fight back. I miss those adventures. I still have old notebooks where I wrote my dreamed-up characters down, describing their powers, even sketching them. I saved the world hundreds of times.

As an adult and as a father I enjoy writing at my breakfast table as it allows me to look out upon our backyard and see my daughters playing outside. Sometimes they are practicing soccer. Sometimes they are just singing and dancing. But occasionally I see them running around with and speaking to others that only their eyes can see. Their adventures sound more like Nancy Drew mysteries or Harry Potter tales because they actually read things besides comic books (unlike their dad in his youth). And I smile because imagination lives!

This is the message I try to pass on to young activists. Speaking out against oppression and fearful hatred is key. Critical refusal in the face of injustice is essential. But we must have the ability to imagine something different and imagine ourselves working to build that something different. We draw from the prophetic aspect of our religious traditions—and rightly so—but we must also draw from the creation narratives of our faiths as well.

I have long been drawn to the activism of the 1960s in the US. Names like Martin King, Ella Baker, Stokely Carmichael, Bayard Rustin, Cesar Chavez, and Dolores Huerta were taught to me as a kid and they have walked with me in my cloud of witnesses ever since. Through them and other activists I learned of the phrase "Power to the People." As a child I might have amended that to say, "Superpower to the People!" as I flew around sad trees trying to uplift the world.

But while in the US we spoke of "Power to the People," at the same time in France, a popular phrase of activists and artists was *L'imagination au pouvoir!* "Power to the imagination!"

It is true. There is so much power in our imaginations. It's there that I learned to be brave. And it's there that I believe we can draw plans to bravely build something new around poverty and homelessness.

What follows is a complex dance about a complex aspect of our lives together. Perhaps there are three "dancing couples" in this book that are seeking to keep the rhythm and not step on each other's toes, while trying to make something beautiful.

The first dance is between reality and imagination. Like my childhood games, which were housed in my head, heart, and in the world around me, this book dances between painfully real experiences that I had and witnessed while working and walking on the streets, and imaginary acts that are perhaps my way of processing what I've seen. This portion of the book is told in verse as I have long attempted to process life through poetry. Maybe it's more than processing though—maybe it's prayer and hope.

I'll leave you to decide what's real and what is imagined.

Secondly the story is a dance between the two literary genres featured in the book—poetry and prose. The poetry is a novel-in-verse and it tells a Mosaic story of liberation. The prose is a theological reflection on that journey and the journey that we all find ourselves on. Together, they form a *theopoetic*. I do so wish

I could take credit for this amazing word, which like all the best art may be interpreted and defined in a range of ways. I see it as meaning the inspiring intersection of art and theology. An effort to do theological work from a poetic paradigm rather than exclusively in a scientific, legal, or over-explanatory way.

Finally, you may choose to read *The Bottom: A Theopoetic of the Streets* with either practical or spiritual eyes (though preferably both). Perhaps you will enter these pages and allow yourself to be heartbroken and moved by the tragedy of homelessness. Maybe this will lead you to add your hands to the heavy (yet doable) lift that it will take to bring about an end to chronic homelessness in our society. Or you might engage the text from a spiritual perspective. In the writing, I found that in many ways the outward and downward journey of the main character transfigured unintentionally into a type of spiritual allegory. Here the hero's journey is downward—where life, and freedom, and God are to be found.

Maybe these ways of reading will dance in and out of vision for you.

However you receive this little book, please know of my deep gratitude for your reading it.

One final story of preface: I shared an early version of this project with a gentleman who has had lots of success in the publishing world. He was generous with his time and feedback. As we were talking though, he paused, and I could tell he was weighing whether or not he should share his final suggestion. He finally does and says that, "The book might be more successful and gain a wider audience if you were to take out the protest parts and all of the Black stuff."

I immediately flashed back to a conversation with my dear sister, the brilliant Ruth Naomi Floyd, in which she talked about temptations and the difficult journey of the critical artist. She shared an image that I have never forgotten, saying that, "It might be beautiful, and it might have Tiffany's diamonds on it, but it's still a handcuff if you can't be who you are."

The temptation to ascend upwards towards more power and money and influence is an ever-present pull away from who we are and what we wish to produce as artists—indeed as humans.

Much of what follows is messy. A lot of this was uncomfortable to write and dream (and some was uncomfortable to witness). Yet, so much of the point of the story is related to freedom. I wanted to write this free so that others might be free. Thus, I give it away freely.[3]

the bottom: a theopoetic of the streets

a preface in verse—the burning bush

I have always been enchanted by lines that are gray
sfumato[4] blurred borders between the now and the not yet
the real and the surreal
the hyperreal
the imagined.

Some realities are self-constructed presenting what we want
    others to see.
Susan Howatch calls these "Glittering Images."[5]

Some realities are projected onto others disallowing them to be
    free.
My father called this being Black in America.

And some realities are not yet.
Our children will call that home.

What follows is a true story
or it could be
will be

I write it in dust on the ground
Free
like liberated poetry

And I give it all away
like fire giving warmth
fire giving light
fire burning a palace to the ground.

Everyone has a burning bush moment.
Yet very few of us pause
remove our sandals
and look into the fire.

Fewer still listen to the call
coming from within the miracle.
And it is the rare individual who overcomes themselves
and actually answers it.

The desert journey from enkindled calling to liberating plagues
must be trod very carefully
while dancing freely.
My feet have walked this path
burned from the sand
bloody from the stones.

Migrated from careless personal *ascent*
to careful anonymous *descent*.

I write this
in story
in song
in graffiti
in poem
in prayer

I write it in dust on the ground
Free
like liberated poetry
And I give it all away

that you may find the flame in your own life
and follow its call.

That you will go out under the humble veil of anonymity and
shake down the walls of whatever Egypt you're living in.
That you can help
people (and perhaps yourself) cross into freedom in small or big
    ways.
And dance by the sea.

Explicit.[6]

reflections from the bottom

All liberating efforts—whether undertaken by activists, politicians, scholars, or artists—must be simultaneously grounded in both a "concrete now" as well as the beneath-the-soil "not yet" seedling. It is both historical and constructive— something like the perennial flower whose past deaths are as integral to the story as its future blooming. It is a chronologically and existentially liminal space—something akin to Pac's *Rose that Grew from Concrete*.[7]

When thinking of the liberative task, I first look to the brilliant Stephen Ray's articulation of one of the goals of Black Liberation Theology as being a "reconstruction of the center."[8] This alludes to the painful reality that people of African descent (or ascent as the great James Spady would say)[9] have for too long in too many places navigated life from the margins of society.

Our experience is marginalized, and we exist in the margins of influence and control far from the center. Yet, we seek not to displace the existing white (male, straight, Christian, able-bodied, cis-gendered) power structure, but rather to introduce other marginalized voices into the center as well. a theology of the bottom continues that project (while adding in class, economic hierarchies, and literal physical spaces) and asks that those on the top in the high-rises and high towers—those in the center—descend to the street and to the margins to work for change from there.

the exodus—the end

(October 4th—Year Two)

We marched. And we sang.
Seeing the water to our left and to our right.
Crossing a blue bridge bearing the name of the intellectual bridge
    himself
Franklin.[10]
Connecting Science and Magic
Enlightenment and Revolution
Pennsylvania and New Jersey

For us connecting an old world and a new reality
Only smiles as "the housed" locked arms with women and men
    who had been living on the streets and in shelters.
We sat and learned together in class earlier that week.
The "Order of Anonymous Beggars" as they came to be called
fell in behind us.

And now we marched and sang.
Each one wearing a shirt with the red fox and black bird symbol
    on our chest.
Symbols are important

as are acts.

And we marched. And we sang.
Someone shouted:

"We are the Exodus!"

Or are we the plague?

Our Red Sea crossing turned into another Bloody Sunday on the
Pettus Bridge.[11]
No easy walks to freedom.
Songs turned to prayers and words turned to screams
as clubs and tear gas and water hoses beat us back over the
bridge
back into the city
back into reality.
Theirs.

No more marching. No more songs.
Only screams almost drowned out by sirens.
We sat down, tucked our knees into our chests and covered our
heads.
We trained for this.
The ghosts of Bayard and Mohandas stood by, nodding in cautious
approval.[12]

I hear the clicks of metal handcuffs
the zips of zip ties.
And just like we practiced we repeat phrases of hope
as we walk by the cameras to the waiting police vans.

I touch the back of my head
and bring my tattooed and scraped arm back in front of my face
I see the red blood
And then the tears of my students
and the tears of the officers
and the indifferent unsurprised look of a homeless brother
named Aaron as he is picked up and slammed to the ground.
He's slept on the streets.
"What's being thrown down into a puddle of disappointment
one more time?"

Cameras caught it all.

Eyes that had been closed for the entire twelve months of our
    campaign—
not in prayer like the marchers, but in sleep and carelessness—
were now being opened.
Teenagers being beaten as they marched for those trapped in
    homelessness and poverty.
Somewhere the girls and boys who felt the sting of the water
    hoses,
the unrestrained teeth of the German Shepherds in Birmingham[13]
The salt marchers[14]
The brave ones who graced Tiananmen Square[15]
all scream from the other side, feeling the hopeful pain of this
    moment.

This is both Exodus and final plague.
Red Sea and a Pesach without doorposts.

Before I close my eyes in unconsciousness I see a woman named
Mira[16]
whose exposed arms betray a burn victim's scars.
She goes unnoticed as always
dancing her way across the bridge
in a free madness.

the bottom—the beginning

(May 9th—Year One)

All storms begin with single drops falling down
flying
from clouds
This is my downward descent.
There are other flights told by other souls.
This is but one.

The catalyst for my own personal exodus,
the first of three burning bushes in my life,
was a nineteen-year-old student in one of my classes.

On Friday mornings I taught a course called
"Religious Dissents" RELS 187

Good Fridays. Shabbat Days. Jummah Days

We wrestled with
figures and movements
within and without
major world religions that dissented from the popular
and moved towards more radically loving postures.

On Friday afternoons I taught another class I had only recently
    developed
"A Theology of the Bottom" RELS 215

Calvary.[17] Kabbalat Shabbat.[18] Jummah Mubarak[19]

Rather than a top-town theology

formed by credentialed scholars
or consecrated religious officials
in high ivory towers
and unwelcoming churches
a theology of the bottom is meant to be more organic
from the people
by the people
radically democratic.

And not just from the bottom in its sources—
But in experience too.
It's about those of us in the gutter.
All who are about that life.
About that death.
Nas called it "Street Dreams"[20]
Pac called it "THUG Life"[21]
A liberation theology.

One definition of liberating work is
reconstructing the center.
I teach my students:

"You see this piece of notebook paper?
Outside of this red line...these are the margins.
Nothing is written in the margins.
The holes are punched in the margins.
We doodle in the margins.
It seems inconsequential.
The most important work is done in the center of the page.
Not in the margins.
Class, this is where we get the term 'marginalized.'

This is the experience of many in our society.
Inconsequential. Away from the center.

Liberative efforts must work to reconstruct the center[22]
and bring the voices of and experiences of the marginalized to
the middle of the paper."

"But why 'the bottom'?" a student asks.

And I tell a story that is forgotten a little bit more every year.
We apologize
trying to make it right.
These buildings of our university
that we study in, live in
displaced a wonderful neighborhood comprised of
Black bodies.
The sisters and brothers who lived there and loved there
affectionately called it
"The Bottom."[23]

That neighborhood is no longer here.

Bulldozed and erased from the collective history
Urban Renewal
Forgotten a little bit more every year.
They whisper through artists like Freeway, Meek, Eve, The Roots,
and Beanie Sigel:[24]

Beanie talkin' 'bout grinding from the bottom only to make it...to
the bottom[25]

I thought maybe, if I'm articulating this theology from a top
school
in what was once The Bottom
then, let's call it that.
And bring theology back to the bottom.

reflections from the bottom

The story of many contemporary urban universities is a story of displacement. For all of the tremendous good that so many schools do through their groundbreaking research, the provision of healthcare, and the daily education of individuals, there are very often rarely-spoken-of stories of not-so-good that have been literally buried beneath the bricks of their campuses. The vibrant neighborhood that once stood on the northern end of our campus was nicknamed by its residents, "The Bottom." This is in great part why I have decided to call this project "a theology of the bottom."

We use words like "gentrification" to describe the fairly quick dismissal we give to families and histories only to replace them with dormitories, research buildings, and retail stores, which on one hand increases the value of a space, lowers crime rates, attracts new businesses to an area, yet on the other displaces families who in many cases had lived in those homes for multiple generations. This is by no means only the work of colleges and universities. Ask Native and Indigenous populations. Ask colonized people-groups who have lost home and language and loved ones. They/we are displaced and moved to the margins. Moved from The Bottom to the bottom.

Then what is our responsibility to a complex tragedy already done? The politicians and leaders who made those decisions— perhaps with good intentions, or perhaps not—are no longer around. "We did not cast them to the bottom!" "We did not throw dirt on their caskets at the bottom!" "We did not lay bricks for the build upwards from the bottom!"

The response need not be one of guilt, but of an incarnational compassion. And we must wonder: Should we tear down inaccessible towers? Should we open up our doors and bring others up? Should we walk downstairs and be with?

midian

These classrooms were once off limits to folks who look like me.
Stories are told of how the first Black students were admitted to
    this school,
but classmates didn't want to see their faces
or hear their voices.
So a chair and desk were
set up
just outside of the classroom.
The margins of the paper.
We had to sit there. Silenced.
Struggling to see the board while remaining unseen.[26]

I do not forget that while standing in the front of a room I was
    once banned from.

My student asks her first of two questions that day. Both
    important. First question:

"Professor, can we have class outside today?"

Sometimes all it takes to start a revolution is a question.

Her second question would be my first burning bush.
Perhaps something within me knew this was coming
as I removed my shoes to feel the cool of the grass when we got
    outside.

Holy Ground

Her face took on an expression of humility before she spoke up.
    Second question:

21

"Professor, I have been thinking about this class and your current
    book project—
your 'theology of the bottom'? And...well...
How can you—or any of us—speak about and teach about those
    on the bottom,
if we have never been there ourselves?
There seems to be the potential for an inauthenticity or a
    distance from—like—full reality."

It isn't simply the leaves of the bush that are burned
(though not consumed)
in these holy and direction-changing moments
but it is also the beholder whose life is singed.

Are you missing the bushes set about your path my friend?
Are hands over your ears keeping the right questions from
    touching your mind
and touching your heart?

After class I entered my office
my cell
with chapel-like windows of stone
hundreds of accumulated books
dozens of collected awards.
And I fall into a squeaky brown leather chair.

I sit high
high above the streets which I study.

Who the hell does she think she is?

my male fragility
my ego
my identity

"How can you—or any of us—speak about and teach about the
    bottom,
if we have never been there ourselves?"

How can I write about
the bottom—the street
when my office is two stories above them?

A thought.
An excited nervousness.
This feels right.
This feels right now

I remembered that in one week my semester would end
and my sabbatical would begin.

Out of the palace
into Midian.

reflections from the bottom

Must one be "of" that which he or she is studying or researching? Is it not possible to intellectually engage and speak of a subject without having originated in that space? I have been holding a question: What might be the difference between a Poverty Theology or a Homelessness Theology, and a theology of the bottom? I answer this with two further questions: From where is the theology originating, where is it being put in practice, and by what means? In other words, where is the theologian working? Literally (in one's office or on the streets) and figuratively (from a top-down salvific posture or from a mutually liberative one).

The notion is similar to the concept of how one engages scripture. Individuals are taught to consider "what we are bringing to the text" and to consider how who/what/where we are may impact how we read holy scriptures—and indeed "do religion." Yet, there is a mobility possible in exegetical[27] reading. In other words, one can draw forth something from scripture and then draw forth something completely different by considering how another from a different social location might interpret it. Perhaps we need to not just move, but we need to move downward in our reading and practice.

Must one be "of" that which he or she is studying or researching...or caring for, or serving? I suppose the answer is no, they don't have to. But to do it well and with authentic love, they should try to bridge any distance there is. They should descend palatial stairs like Moses. Old preachers used to say, "A shepherd ought to smell like their sheep!"

joy in the leaving

(July 20th—Year One)

there is joy in the leaving
an awful joy
it was an odd thing
the excitement I felt.

L'imagination au pouvoir[28]

There is joy in the leaving...
an awesome joy

A freedom from the demands of my professional and social life
Led out of bondage.
Not like slavery
but the bondage that is the palace.

Friend, I tell you to leave.
Jump out of the first-floor windows of the palace and run.
We are free out here.
Richer and stronger
and certainly free.

Ingratitude is among the greatest human tragedies
and I don't mean to wear that.
How could I consider a life teaching and serving
at one of the world's finest schools to be bondage?
I loved my job. It made me fairly wealthy
and this wealth afforded me privilege
and this privilege allowed me to go almost anywhere
do almost anything...

...like leave my reality for
the surreality of the streets.
Hyperreality.

I began part-time (my privilege again)
I would spend my days in disguise on the streets.
Returning back to my own bed at night.

Disguises are complicated things.
I have a confession.
I Am
a comic book geek. I grew up reading them and I still read them.
X-Men spoke to a little Black mutant like me.[29]
Wasn't until I was on the streets that I finally understood
why so many heroes wear masks and costumes.
They protect Lois and Mary Jane, yes.[30]
If enemies know their true identities then the
families of heroes might be in danger.
Thus, they don't know he's Clark. They don't know he's Peter.[31]

But that is not the only why.
With the mask, Bruce Wayne escapes the world of the Billionaire
    Playboy.[32]

I escape as well.
I'm no hero.
Was never trying to be.
And I know too much to dare be proud.
And I'm known too much to be a hero.
The true heroes remain unknown. Even after the good.

My disguise? A large black hoodie in memory of Trayvon.[33]
Dark black sunglasses to hide my tears.
And a large backpack to carry my things and my books.

I left.

Walked down the stairs from my townhouse and went into the
desert that is the city.

Come with.

reflections from the bottom

I would encourage you to just go. Make your first trip out during the daytime. Bring no notes. This shouldn't be an ethnographic project, but an incarnational one. Walk the streets. Walk in the posture of a student. Pay attention to what you are feeling. Are you nervous or afraid? Why? What are you afraid of and from where does that fear originate?

Try not to pretend or act "how you think folks on the streets act." Just be. And don't force any conversation. Indeed, I'd recommend just walking. Pass by. Be transient. But spend some real time out there. Hours and not minutes. This is incarnational love. Being with rather than just sending donations.

Once fear has been shed, visiting the street may be a profoundly spiritual experience. Certainly eye-opening. Awakening even. Being in solidarity with is a deeply spiritual experience. Incarnationally loving is a devoutly religious experience. Entering into the reality of the suffering of others is certainly a step towards enlightenment. Towards love. And a theology of the bottom asks right at the outset that one come down.

We are taught through so many of our religious and spiritual traditions that the path should lead us "up the mountain" and heavenward. And yet, and I speak as a Christian here, Christ's path shows that preceding the ascension, one must descend down to be with humanity.

So much of Christianity has floated upward away from this truth. We preach prosperity and security and a faux purity while the life and witness of the homeless Nazarene bears witness against us.

cool limp

(July 20th—Year One)

Growing up I took on a fake limp
to be cool.
Gwendolyn told us "we real cool"[34]
Less limp more of a slight dip.
Denzel Cool.

My first day on the street
I instinctively began to walk with a limp
shuffling more than walking.
I mumbled to others as they passed and constantly looked down.
Shame on me
for the stereotypes I took on that first day out on the street.
Homelessness is
far more complicated and diverse than the "bum" or "crazy bag
    lady" images
we perpetuate.
I should know better.
I teach this.
But what did I know of the street?

Was never that guy
to take a peek at my reflection
in the windows of stores as I passed them by,
but insecurity led me to gaze to my right and
see the mockery that I was.

Woooooooo!
Insecurity is a hell of a drug!

I stood up straight, lost the limp and just kept walking.

I found a small playground in one of the residential
    neighborhoods downtown.
Sat down on one of the benches.
Feet tired already.
Questioning decisions
Replaying conversations.

Dog walkers.
Black nannies watching white children.

We real cool.

A white woman pushing a stroller aims towards the benches.

I move and
cross the park.

I know this feeling.
It's the daily smalling Black men do with nervous white folks.
They clutch their purse
and we get smaller
or cross the street
or quiet our voices
or code switch.

I cross the park.

And sit with it.

"Your playing small does not serve the world!"[35]

Friend, why are you shrinking yourself because of the white gaze

or the male gaze
or the straight gaze
or the Christian gaze
or the "normal gaze"?[36]

I sit on another bench and gaze at nothing, everything.

Time moves extremely slowly on the streets.

With a tender care
a dad dries off the wet seat of the swings
before pushing his daughter.
Another mother and child join them.
I hear their entire conversation.
The cost of daycare in the fall,
vacation plans,
one of the women's younger brother's wedding,
the graphic design business run out of his home.

Bored, I began to look around.
I had never really stopped to notice how green this little park
    was.
I saw a worm.
This made me smile.
Slowly moving across the ground in what Kirk Jones would call "A
    Savoring Pace."[37]

My older sister used to call me a worm.
Makes me laugh thinking about that.
"Bow down to me, worm!" she'd say jokingly—sort of.

Never totally understood why they called Rodman the worm,
but that cat could pull a board down.
Never was afraid to be himself.[38]

I get lost on a tangent.
A train of thought
subway of memories
while staring at a worm on the ground.
And a full hour passes by
I return to the present only after my foot falls asleep
Shifting to another position
another worm catches my eye

These forgotten friends
literally lower than dirt.
So important for the earth
yet overlooked and thought of as disgusting.

Gardeners know.
They do the unseen work
beneath the surface
helping the entire garden to live.

I lay down with my chest facing the ground to get a closer look.
Only in hindsight can I imagine how I must have looked to the
    others in the park.
I now understand why they put their children back in the strollers
    and
walked away.

I stare for twenty minutes.
Details.
Saw a lot of details that I usually miss.

My legs began to stiffen so I moved around
shifted my weight
realized that my jeans were now wet on the bottom.
I got up and limped away.

reflections from the bottom

There is a trap in all of this. The temptation to romanticize the experience on the street by imagining there are "angels in disguise"[39] waiting to dispense wisdom or that sitting on concrete will bring some kind of enlightenment. These lamp posts are no Bodhi Trees.[40] There is certainly a freedom that comes with leaving the top—no doubt. And this is profoundly spiritual, but coming down to the bottom is not the goal. This is not salvation or awakening. And it is terrible. Absolutely terrible.

My conversations with sisters and brothers on the streets reveal both the difficulty of finding food, shelter, a place to relieve oneself, let alone the potential dangers on the street and in the shelter system. These conversations also betray the boredom that many feel. The silence and lack of fellow interlocutors can be maddening. A kind of walking solitary confinement. Yes, that's it. It is less boredom than it is isolation.

One of the goals of a theology of the bottom is the building of community—especially the bringing of isolated individuals into communities. This is liberation from isolation. This is liberation from the sin of leaving neighbors alone. Note that isolation plagues the high-rises and towers up above as well. The academy, the suburbs, wealth, and security, do not protect us from the pain of loneliness and lack of connection.

The walk downstairs and into community is a powerful and life-giving journey, but don't skip down here with a smile on your face. Walk with trepidation. Walk with faith in knowing God is with you. But with an appropriate reverence for the pain you will see.

paulo, rumi, boff, and francis (preface to the plagues)

(March 7th—Year Two)

In the months and minutes
leading up to the
plagues and the exodus
Twice a week we gathered.
Women and men who were navigating homelessness—
(and we never called anyone simply "homeless." It's not who we
   are, it's something we experience.)
Women and men who were navigating homelessness—
(and, by the way, don't we all experience homelessness of one
   sort or another at some point in our lives?)
Women and men who were navigating homelessness,
along with college and high-school students and parents and
   friends and allies,
gathered together to learn
with each other and from each other
We formed circles like Paulo Freire.[41]

Some called it "Street College"
An older sister called it "New Freedom School"
One brother called it "The Yeshiva Without Walls."

I wanted to be the Rumi in this Madrassa.[42]
Teaching madly with love.
Madness in the words of sojourners discharged from institutions
   long ago
Madness is the dreams of creating something new.

I did what I have always done.

Teach.
For years I taught at the university on the west side
For days I taught at the benches downtown.

When not teaching I extended hands like
Anonymous Beggars.

I wanted to be Leonardo Boff in this Base Community[43]
Liberating with liberation theology
The freedom of a professed religious
The freedom of a former monk

I taught those who others had given up on
Bringing the theology from the towers of my university
down to the bottom.

this is a theology of the bottom.

always lowercase.

I wanted to be Francis preaching to the birds.[44]
And they'll fly to higher ground—higher than where I was
high enough to be free
high enough to be free.

reflections from the bottom

The incarnation of Christ is in many ways the icon of what we mean by a theology of the bottom and a theopoetic of the streets—His "coming down" (if I may present heaven as being "up there") to be in humanity with us. Wrapping words around the Divine is dangerous in that it always falls short. Yet, if I may I would say that the descending salvific act of Christ is poetic in its love. It's hard to describe, it doesn't play by cosmic grammatical rules, and it's...the Word come to us.

This beautiful descending image exists in other faith traditions as well. Moses leaving Pharaoh's palace to be with the enslaved Hebrews. Muhammad leaving the comforts of life in Mecca for a cave in Mount Hira and then to live in Medina. The Buddha leaving the privilege of not knowing suffering to walking through it to enlightenment. a theology of the bottom asks for the forfeiture of privilege—at least in part—and for us to come down with those who are navigating homelessness and poverty, so that we might co-work for liberation and co-experience resurrection.

The coming-down process must occur in the teaching specifically. Thus, creating radically democratic classroom spaces where all are teachers and all are students. Perhaps there are times and spaces where the "top down" teaching model is the best practice, but that is not within this theological house. Our method demands taking seriously the experience and brilliance of all who gather with a desire to mutually learn and mutually liberate. Inevitably, when the educational direction of a group of learners is opened up to that community, the learning leads to direct action that will seek to bring about real change. This ultimately is one of the goals of this theology—learning for the sake of a center-reconstructing change.

plague—caterpillars

(March 9th—Year Two)

Wait.
An overlooked unmentioned part of life on the streets.
Wait in line at the soup kitchen
Wait in line to check in at the shelter
Wait for the rain to stop
Wait for the SSI check to come
Wait for my caseworker to wrap up her phone call
Wait to die
Wait to live.

We waited for just the right evening
Had to be
warm enough for us all to stay outside.
Can't sneak out of shelters at night.
Doors closed.
That night was dropping to 49 degrees.
Folks on the street always know what the weather's gonna be.
That's cold, but not unbearable for us to sleep or act in.

Three plagues in one night
'Cause, well, tomorrow isn't promised.

We completed the "art installation" under the cover of night
Four dark hours.

God ain't use no swords or guns for His plagues.
Just art. The poetry of nature. The pain of the different.

Peace God! Strike again!

Ten cans of spray paint
Two stacks of scrap plywood and cardboard
Ten large pre-painted sheets.
Twenty beating hearts that were tired of being overlooked and
    dehumanized.

We began slowly on the sidewalks in front of City Hall
and the large offices and banks downtown.
Hard to move fast with trench foot.[45]

The city's Mural Arts Program provided the inspiration and the
    materials.[46]
They beautify the city and tell its stories.
A simple effort that has made a profound impact.
And because of the numerous awards and grant money they've
    received over the years
no one would've suspected them of aiding us in our nocturnal
plaguing efforts.

They didn't
wouldn't
see us.
Many experiencing
homelessness
sleep in the plaza in front of the building which is
home
to the Mayor and City Council.
No one would notice a few more of us.

Vamos. Yalla.

We lay down and slid into donated sleeping bags
restlessly pretending to rest.
Like worms

slugs
no—caterpillars!
With one arm stretched out from under the blanket
out from the sleeping bags
we write words and numbers to cover the sidewalks of the
four square blocks upon which City Hall stood
In red and blue spray paint we write.
Fumes hitting us.
Spray paint hitting the pavement as we inch along still in bags.
    We write:

"No Living Wage"
"Lack of Affordable Housing"
"Poor Integration of Returning Vets"
"Domestic Abuse"
"Natural Disaster"
"Lack of Insurance"
"Discrimination"
"Ableism"

"14,986 homeless in Philadelphia this year"
"5000 on any given day are homeless"

Cause and Effect.
We came up with forty different causes.

And then quotes, song lyrics, and prayers
all concerning homelessness and poverty
filled the space that would soon be traversed by dress shoes and
    high heels.
All in spray paint.

One of us wrote memorized words by the Indian poet
Mirabai

on the ground in front of a high-rise building that housed both an outpatient mental health treatment facility and a bank.
She adapted the poem's final words to say:

"And everyone says WE are mad."[47]

reflections from the bottom

Dorothy Day was known to often quote Fyodor Dostoevsky and say, "We shall be saved by beauty."[48] The role of art in revolution is often overlooked, perhaps because it is seen as ugly to those in power. But to the soon-to-be-liberated, to those of us on the bottom, all freedom art is beautiful. The art of the Harlem Renaissance, *La Négritude*, the Black Arts Movement—all were crucial to the larger Black liberative arc in the US.

Art "tells the truth slant" as the great Emily Dickinson poem says.[49] Art can also tell the truth hard. And there are times when the words on the margins of the page are illegible to eyes that don't want to read them. Thus, sometimes it's the doodles and scribbles right across the middle of the page that gain the attention of the reader.

It is important for revolutionary literature—writing that seeks to move and revolve both hearts and societies—to not only be written clearly, but to be written or rather shared artistically. Through visual art, film, music, comics, and even poetry.

plague—foxes and birds

(March 10th—Year Two)

We are split in two.

"This is madness,"
Someone whispers.
"Nah. I've seen madness young buck..."
says the old vet cool limping along
from an old wound that never healed right.

We are split in two.

Worms—no—caterpillars tagging in front of City Hall
and another crew hitting up the churches.
Every
single
one
of the downtown churches.

When there was no one walking or driving by,
they placed a small sculpture on the steps in front of the door.
During the three days prior
we used
plywood and
cardboard attempting to replicate the work of the formerly
    unhoused artist named
Matthew Works.[50]
He created,
while he was on the street,
a small cardboard congregational-style church.
On the front of it hung a large metal padlock.

On the sides were quotes from scripture referencing God's love
  for the poor.
On the inside was the Holy Spirit.
The lock on the front of the sculpture spoke to how many
  churches lock their doors
while those of us on the streets
freeze and starve to death.

We made thirty replicas of this prophetic artwork.
Each pair that dropped off the churches left a handwritten letter
  explaining what it was.
A gift—an offering they called it.

At the churches that had soup kitchens, evening shelters, or
  programs for individuals navigating homelessness,
a picked flower was given along with the gift.
The places that did nothing or were especially hostile to us on the
  street?
Those sculptures were given with a cut piece of a thorn bush
  and a note that directed them to the back outside wall of the
  church where we wrote in red spray paint:

The foxes have holes
and the birds of the air have nests
but the Son of man
hath nowhere to lay his head.[51]

There was a younger sister named Habibti who was with us at our
  gatherings
in the days leading up to the plague.
Upon hearing this verse for the first time
she drew an image of a fox and a bird moving together.
When we saw the image that she drew,
we thought it would make a good symbol for our efforts,

for the outdoor school that we had begun,
and of our hopes.

"Symbols are important," I taught them that day
on the benches in front of the public library.
"Some symbols strike terror
others inspire hope.
What about this fox and bird that Habibti drew?
Terror or Hope?"

We took a knife and cut the image out of a piece of cardboard
making a type of stencil allowing us to reproduce the fox and bird
    image on every wall that we tagged.

When you have nothing more to lose,
Why stop?
People with nothing left to lose are the most dangerous.
Or the most free?

After City Hall and after the churches, we spread out
and ran alone knowing that we would meet at the designated
    spot by
the river at sunrise,
which was coming in sixty minutes.
During these solo trench-foot sprints,
with the rest of the city asleep,
cats took the remaining spray paint and ended up tagging
cars
stop signs
the windows of stores
and nearly every and any thing with a surface.
I wasn't meaning to do all of this.
Was this the Holy Spirit tearing free
or an uncontrollable madness split in two?

Or just anger and pain meeting catharsis?

On each car, sign, or window we wrote the words
"Free the Homeless"
"Fix the Shelters" or
"We are Human too"
always adding either the word "shame," "care," or "madness."
And those who couldn't write or who didn't have paint just spat
or pissed on them.

Split in two.

A few of us got arrested at this point.
Each one arrested separately from one another.
Each with not a single f*** left to give.

reflections from the bottom

We disrupt not for the sake of disruption. Not for the attention. Indeed we seek to counter the attention-seeking top. Rather we disrupt to draw attention to suffering. Philadelphia prophet Shane Claiborne says, "We risk arrest to arrest the attention of society."[52] This was the point of sit-ins at the kitchen counters, die-ins in the street, people chaining themselves to bulldozers. The microphone is high up on the stage. We on the bottom aren't even in the crowd to yell to the stage. We are outside of the arena. How can we be heard, but by pulling the fire alarm?

And we do this with great grief. I'll speak personally here — my family didn't raise me to be "disrespectful." And yet sometimes the urgency of life calls for a death of manners. Thus, a theology of the bottom moves with a method that isn't seeking attention, but rather is seeking change "by any means necessary"[53] short of a violence that turns us into the monsters we seek to convert.[54] It begs for praxis. An intersection between theory and practice. The word "praxis" seems to not have enough life-or-death urgency behind it — it doesn't communicate the gritty, enduring desperation that many of us out here feel. It's more than theory and practice; it's theory and a hungry action.

plague—the river turned to blood

(March 10th—Year Two)

The final act was done by brothers and sisters who,
while not living on the street, were certainly a part of the
    movement.
Climbing to the tops of three parking garages right in the middle
    of
the city
they unraveled three large painted banners,
murals
and hung
them from the side of the parking lot.
The lots were on the corners of the three busiest intersections
    ensuring maximum visibility.
The community members who worked on the murals produced
    some of the most amazing art I had ever seen.
No words.
Simply images of homeless women and men
Real people
Bodies lying uncomfortably on wooden benches.
Open hands holding pennies.
And careless onlookers.
The message was clear:
We as a society need to care more about people on the streets,
do more to help,
and work to free them from a cycle of poverty that is hindering
    them—us
from being their best selves.

These images hung above.
The sculptures stood on steps.

The smell of fresh spray paint filled the air.

We art-bombed the city.
The first night.

"This s*** ain't comin' off!" Aaron repeated.

Graffiti was our preferred medium and it made sense.
During the late 1960s and 1970s with the advent of Hip Hop,
graffiti emerged as a powerful way for young women and men to
    express themselves
during a time when art programs were being cut in many urban
    school districts.
Young people forgotten and overlooked
Writing one's name on the side of a subway was a way of being
seen and heard
at a time when we felt
overlooked, ignored, and given up on.

The notion of being a large-scale graffiti artist first truly emerged
    in
Philadelphia.
Lotta firsts there.
Midnight walks
reveal the ghosts of
"Cornbread" and "Cool Earl"
Backpacks
Hats turned around
Gloves with the fingertips cut off.
They and our people might often not be seen
but you'll see their names and messages on
bridges, overpasses, buses, subways
and even the underside of a TWA jet.[55]
Great story there.

Graffiti is art,
illegal art
but art nonetheless.
Art that speaks
for folks who don't feel heard.
We have been screaming from the streets for years.
Sounds like whispers to those who walk by.

The ugliest part for us was that the morning after these first
    plagues,
people would put a greater value on their cars, windows, and
    sidewalks
than on the message or the people who sent the message.
Childish
This is America.[56]

We tried to communicate a message, not to destroy.
God's first or second or third plague
could have been the only plagues had Pharaoh just listened.

The not-yet-dry paint on windows was scraped and power-washed
    away by sanitation workers
(though not before rush hour and the morning news reports
    covered it)
who were just one paycheck away from being on the streets
with us.
Sidewalk paint was gonna be there for a while.

The church sculptures—
for some reason most of those made it inside.
Many were publicly displayed in sanctuaries.
The Cathedral Dean and the
Priests in the Basilica placed theirs
on their altar

for all to see.
That's Eucharist.
God bless 'em.
And three churches were so moved by the replicas of
Matthew's work
they decided to keep their doors open
all day and every night
to anyone who needed shelter.
Pharaoh was beginning to lose his grip.

After we finished,
the un-arrested
went to the banks of the river
to wash the paint off of our clothes and our bodies.
For those of us who don't want to or aren't allowed to use the
    shelter system,
this is the only place,
besides a public bathroom sink, that we can wash up.

There is a thick quiet around one who knows they're about to be
arrested.
This was to be my first time.
I'd been stopped by cops in
every city
I'd ever been in for
walking or driving
while Black.
But never straight up arrested.

The early morning sirens that we heard from a distance grew
closer and closer
until city police rushed to the bridge that we were bathing
    beneath.
Two television cameras and a network helicopter captured the

"raid" live for viewers to see.

We anticipated the media's presence
needed them to get the story out
needed them to keep the cops accountable[57]
thus we were only a little bit insecure,
about the
imperfect bodies
that were now being revealed on television.
With feelings somewhere between a second-guessing terror and
    a mischievous amusement
(Get in "good trouble" says John Lewis)[58]
we walked waist deep into the
cold water of the river
then turned around to face the cameras and the policemen.

Bodies that haven't held the gaze of another for years
forfeited their illusionary privacy
revealing hidden tattoos
aged scars
and hairy chests that covered hearts broken long ago.

We were ordered out of the water,
but apparently our nearly naked bodies and trench feet
didn't move fast enough.
The officers began to grab and pull us out.
Aaron didn't like being touched.
When an officer grabbed him by the arm, Aaron pushed him
    down.

Three other cops pulled out their clubs and began to strike him
Even after he lost consciousness
they continued to beat his fifty-two-year-old
Black body

on the edge of the water.
As the water lapped up on the shore it mixed with the
blood that was flowing from the cuts caused by fists and clubs,
pulling the red liquid into the river.

reflections from the bottom

For many of us, being arrested has become a type of sacrament. We feel the same Holy Spirit presence as handcuffs are locked around our wrists that we do in other holy moments. To explain it from a Christian perspective, we drink from the Cup and eat the Bread because Christ did and so that we might be at the table with Him. We are baptized because Christ was, to follow Him. We now are arrested after non-violent resistance for the sake of others...again because Christ too was arrested for our sakes.

Telling stories of "times we got arrested protesting" can veer towards the same goals of old high-school sports glory stories. They can end up being self-serving for a type of street cred rather than God-glorifying and movement-furthering. I share the following story with this caution in mind.

"I want Jesus to walk with me..."

A sister's brave alto solemnly washes over our heads from within the midst of our procession. The cool breeze on this hot Washington DC day carries her words as she begins to sing louder, with a slight variation on the word "walk."

"I want Jesus, to walk with me!"

Holding the pain of the individuals who were advocating for that day, the undying burden of racism in America, and the overwhelming and seemingly endless chaos of that political moment, we all join in the haunting melody of the old spiritual:

"All along this tedious journey...I want Jesus to walk with me."

We step slowly. Slow enough for those on canes to keep up. Slow enough for us to brace ourselves for our imminent arrests. Slow enough to feel the ghosts of past, good-troublemakers walking beside us.

Today, we walk the same stony road that they trod. Soon, we'll face the same chastening rod.

Just an hour before, while getting off the train in Union Station, I touched the humble statue of A. Philip Randolph that greeted us there in the hallway. Then, walking by the Mall, I thought of Bayard's strategizing, Ella's training, and Mahalia's gift of song which blessed this space fifty-five summers ago.

And passing his majestic monument, which now stands as a peaceful convicting sentinel, I thought of Martin's dream and his commitment to putting legs on his faith and walking towards fear and hate with love.

When I was growing up I spent my summers at sleep-away sports camps. One of the potentially slightly exaggerated sports glory stories that I often tell my kids is about a basketball game we were playing against a rival camp during my last summer. I was tall for my age and I loved playing ball. During the first half I was torching these guys. But the ref (in my unbiased opinion) called four quick fouls on me in the third quarter. I sat myself down even though my coach/counselor wanted me to stay in. When my coach came over to me on the bench and asked me what I was doing, I said, "Man, that ref is pickin' on me!"

I was the only Black player, and the largest player on the court that game. And in hindsight I do think he called fouls on me that he wasn't calling on other players. Likewise, when I was fouled I didn't get the calls. As someone who has refereed a lot of youth sports since then, I'm aware that many referees officiate certain players differently, either consciously or unconsciously, for a wide range of reasons. Sometimes it is in an effort to make it fun for all the athletes; thus the stronger players often get refed differently than the weaker ones. Other times a player might remind a ref of a kid they didn't like when they were growing up, so that player is treated differently—intentionally or unintentionally. Likewise, unconscious bias and stereotypes that we hold about certain people-groups can most certainly affect how they are treated on the court or field. Whether this ref didn't like me because of my race, or he was trying to keep it competitive, or he just made some bad calls, I don't know. I do know that I was mad and I didn't want to play anymore.

My coach got right in my face and gave me a brief, but needed, pep talk: "I know it's unfair. I see it. I'm mad, too. But don't stop playing. Your team needs you out there. Get yourself back in that game."

So I got myself back in that game.

We keep marching. Slowly. Nervously. I had risked arrest once before, but not in DC. Not at the White House. Not with media like this watching us. It's easier for me to teach about discrimination; harder to fight against it and risk arrest.

And so I keep marching in Washington. Dreaming, yes, but also marching. Ahead of me is Rev. Dr. William Barber—pastor, prophet, and leader in the Poor People's Campaign (another such march that Martin was planning, just before he was killed). Barber walks cane in hand, Bible in heart, truth in mouth. I look over his shoulder. A crowd of tourists part. Not like the Red Sea, more like onlookers at a funeral procession. Police officers (some mounted on horseback, some dismounting motorcycles, some in cars, others who've been standing with displayed weapons all day) fall into positions they have had to take more and more in this season of demonstration and resistance.

We, too, take our positions. We line up in front of the White House, each holding signs of protest.

We hear voices sing out from those fellow demonstrators who are not risking arrest: "*Ain't gonna let nobody turn me around, turn me around, turn me around. Ain't gonna let nobody turn me around. Gonna keep on walkin'. Keep on talkin'. Marching on to freedom land.*"

A different voice hits our ears. This voice is not sung, but instead is broadcast from the police car that has parked right in front of us. We're told that we are in violation of both federal and DC codes, which prohibit us from demonstrating and not moving from this spot right in front of the White House. This is our first, and then our second, and then our third and final warning.

"If you do not leave the sidewalk immediately, you will be arrested."

"Ain't gonna let no handcuffs turn me around, turn me around, turn me around..."

I'm not saying that all need to risk arrest. That isn't everyone's calling. Nor do we all have the privilege and flexibility to take time off from work and afford the fines that come along with arrest. Yet, it's a lot easier to sit on the bench and complain. Harder to actually take the court. Whether it's protesting and marching or not, consider what putting legs on your faith might look like.

I look to my right and Barber pulls the large cross that hangs around his neck up to his lips and whispers a prayer. My Philadelphia brother Shane Claiborne looks upward in silent petition. Rev. Jim Wallis the Sojourner closes his eyes and prays loud enough for all of us and for his God to hear. My eyes are closed and my thoughts move between praying and wondering what my wife and daughters will think. I then think of Martin, and the sisters and brothers in the SNCC and the SCLC, and the NAACP, and the children of Birmingham and all who were arrested while marching against hate.

King speaks from the past: "This will be the day when all of God's children will be able to sing with new meaning: 'My country, 'tis of thee, sweet land of liberty, of thee I sing. Land where my fathers died, land of the pilgrim's pride, from every mountainside, let freedom ring!'"[59]

I think about King and his two arms of love. The right arm fighting to bring about change, even as it was being bent around his back for arrest. The left arm constantly working for reconciliation and community-building, even with those who were on the opposite side of issues from him.

The officers come to arrest us one by one. I turn around and see the tall pillars of the White House and I make the sign of the cross. I am taken and handcuffed. The officers were all kind. Firm, but kind. And especially gentle with the older protesters. I thank the gentleman who guides me over to be processed. I offer to pray for him. This is King's left hand.

The handcuffs cut into my tattooed wrist, leaving another mark—this one I did not desire. I share a cell with my brother Rev. William Gipson, and two other demonstrators. We chat, trying to keep it loose and distract ourselves from claustrophobia. I think of Martin writing from the Birmingham jail. I think of all the sisters and brothers who look like me and are locked up far longer than the few hours I'd be spending in my cell. I think of all the other clergy and people of faith who walked the same path into cells after demonstrating the last couple of years. Risking arrest has become almost a sacrament for many of us. It is a powerful embodied act of faith, indeed. A powerful act of believing that change can happen. A powerful act of trusting in God. a theology of the bottom does not require arrest. It does ask for action though. Complaining and talking about fouls isn't enough. Get back in the game.[60]

first night out

(July 24th—Year One)

Easy to play homeless when you got a home waiting for you.
Easy to play broke when you got money in the bank and a
    retirement fund.
I spent the first few days on the street
uncomfortable and hungry
but always with a safety net and a hot meal waiting for me at
    home.
This is not incarnation
this is not a theology of the bottom
this is tourism
voyeurism
poverty porn.

Like a short-term missionary
who never learns the local language
or anyone's name.

"I'm sleeping outside tonight."
I chose, others didn't have a choice.
"But where will I sleep?"
A real question many ask themselves every day.

I used to take students to visit shelters
for field trips
I'm not trying to sleep there.
No shelters on this side of town near the universities.
"Parents wouldn't feel too good about a bunch of
winos and bag ladies
wandering around campus would they?

Not good for business,"
I remembered an administrator saying
after a group of
good-hearted students
proposed the idea of
a university-sponsored shelter.[61]

Twenty-four-hour diner that's a few blocks away?
Nah they put folks out
who look homeless.
"Not good for business."

I headed towards an underpass,
for shelter in case it rains again.
In my car this would've taken just ten minutes.
Gonna be more like an hour by foot
and I was ready to lie down and get off my feet.

I pass a bench
Three planks of wood never looked more comfortable.
I pulled my hood all the way up
so that on the outside chance one of my colleagues
or former students walked by
they wouldn't recognize me,
and I went to the bench with the mission of getting some sleep.

I chuckled to myself as my mind
began to play the song
"Nessun Dorma" from the opera *Turandot*.[62]
Sad but true.
On these wooden benches no one sleeps.
They're designed that way.
The little bar in the middle doubles as an elbow rest
and a simple inhibiter to anyone trying to stretch out and sleep.

Not meant to be cruel
but look,
homeless "loitering" is not good for business.
Rather than spending the resources to help get people off the
    streets
and reintegrated back into a society that has marginalized them,
we'd rather spend the money on the barred benches and gates
    that keep unhoused individuals away.

Thus, I was forced to sleep sitting up.
Backpack cushioning my head as it leaned on the back of the
    bench.
Somehow, I managed to doze off...

...only to be awakened by a group of teenagers either
leaving or going somewhere.
Laughs and yells startled me
Drew me back from the escape of sleep.
The group started to walk towards me.
One had a baseball bat,
another had a gasoline container,
another had a lighter.

The one who seemed like their leader said,
"Nah leave him alone. That bum's too big. Not drunk enough.
    Let's keep lookin'."

If you are reading this or listening to this
don't you ever forget how dangerous it is on the street for
people.

And I don't mean gun violence or being mugged or anything like
    that.
I mean for folks who live out here.

This is why no one sleeps.
We might die if we close our eyes
not because of who is sleeping on the next bench over
but because of the folks who don't see us as human.

I sit wide-eyed.
Hands shaking
replaying what just happened
imagining it going differently.
Would I have fought those kids?
Would I have died?
Would I have—

"Yo Professor!" I heard a voice say

It was a brother named Aaron.
I've known him a long time.
He's panhandled on our campus for as long as I've been here.
Friendly—some think that's a part of the hustle.
Nah—he's a decent guy. Just has a story as to why he's out here
    too.

He handed me a cup of coffee.
I have brought this dude like a hundred cups of coffee over the
    years.
Am I too proud to take this one?
I could tell he saw what almost happened with those teen
    terrorists.

He pulled out an extra blanket from his bag and gave it to me.
Aaron ain't know why I was out there, but
he just sat down on the other side of the deterrent bar
on the bench.
Undeterred.

reflections from the bottom

The dangers for individuals who sleep on the street are seldom known and very rarely understood. The misconception that those navigating chronic homelessness are violent is a cruel image that many of us project onto them. We often inaccurately think that all who are on the street are drug addicts or alcoholics. Subsequently, we then associate violence with drug use (except when it's suburban kids and recreational marijuana use by white individuals). Racism and racist stereotypes are also rolled into the fear and disgust many have for folks on the bottom. To be clear, there are of course individuals on the street who are struggling with addictions—around 40% with alcohol (mostly older populations) and 25% with drugs (younger). Yet—and this is key—it is not all. Further, an addiction should never be seen as the totality of who an individual is. It might be one of the root causes of why they are out here. Might even be one of the chains keeping them there. But it isn't who they are. It's an illness.

Our fear of violence *from* them distracts us from the violence done *to* them. Individuals on the street are often a population that lacks the resources to file a complaint or sue. They lack the cultural capital to even be heard. This makes them easy silent targets for many types of assaults. They become the bottom of the bottom. The assault of a scornful look is hard enough to bear.

aaron

(July 24th—Year One—looking back to much earlier)

"Check it. If I beat box and rap for y'all
can you help me out with gettin' somethin' to eat?"

These were the first words I heard Aaron utter some twenty years
    ago.
Young white college kids entertained by this young Black addict
hustlin' for some change
yes to eat
maybe to get another hit.
Probably to get another hit.

And he did beat box.
Somethin' like a poor man's Dougie Fresh
or a poor man's Biz Markie[63]
or just a poor man.

I sat there embarrassed by the white gaze[64]
this invisible force that causes Black folks to overthink behavior
    and perception.
He over there "cooning"[65]
I stopped it by digging in my pockets for money and pulling the
    brother away from
the mockers.

I doubt Aaron remembers this.
He was drunk that day.

Back to the present:
We sat on the bench and Aaron pulled out an old Gideon's Bible[66]

(didn't know they still made those)
He reads a psalm.
I've seen Aaron on these streets for years
never knew about his "religious side."

Amid his addictions
and his hustles
and his homelessness
this cat loves God.

I learned later that his mother was a deaconess
...that his mother was so proud of him when he finished culinary
    school
...that his mother died soon after
...that he drowned that pain with booze
...that his drinking turned into an addiction
...that turned into him missing work
...that turned into him losing his job
...then losing his apartment
...then losing his wife and kids

"F*** is you doing out here Professor?" he said in a voice kinder
    than the words he chose.
"I know you got a home."

He saw me writing and taking notes and
inquired about what I was doing.

Messy.

I had intended to keep my "undercover research"
undercover.
Being studied can make people feel uncomfortable.

I tell him.

"A theology of the bottom huh?
You out here to study us?"
Anger and appreciation in the same sentence
on the same face.

Pause.

"You know for a second, I felt some kinda way
'bout you being out here doin' research,
studying me—like I was a rat or something.
Like you was gonna just write another one of yo' books.
Yeah I read yo' books.
You surprised I can read ain't you?
Oh this N****!
See...that's why I ain't mad you out here.
I want you to go back and tell our story.
Hell, I want you to change our story.
You want to see the bottom?
You ain't nowhere close yet.
The bottom ain't a place.
Well not no more.
The bottom is a life.
You can't get there going undercover.
You can't get there sitting wit a bunch a n***** on the street
You need to get down here yo' self.
I'ma pray that for you.
That God drags yo' a** down to the bottom
then pulls you back up...
and brings the rest of us up with you."

reflections from the bottom

The bottom is not a place. It is a life. The bottom is a holistic life of intersecting systems of oppression and causes of suffering. An important mark of a theology of the bottom is the recognition of the multiple causes of suffering as well as the need for multiple paths to liberation. In many ways this profound point draws from the brilliance of Womanist Theology[67] with its ability to integrate sexism, racism, classism (and other forms of oppressions) into the same space and into the same goal of liberation. This commitment to this multifaceted project must be one of the practical marks of a theology of the bottom. The key difference being, however, *where* this theology is practiced. And by *whom*.

Within his book *Pedagogy of the Oppressed*, Brazilian educational philosopher Paulo Freire[68] challenges academics and educators to take more seriously the intellectual capabilities of the "non-tutored." This also is a Gramscian[69] notion addressing the preexisting education of "popular workers" from the non-classroom or, to borrow a phrase, "the school of hard knocks." It is also connected to the theory of the organic intellectual who, while not having letters after her or his name, is still just as able to do intellectual work and high-level (or in this case beneficently low-level) thinking.

In a very real and moving way Aaron is a powerful intellectual—a theologian even. His "God-talk" and reflections were deep, let alone his mastery of human nature. And the aspects of his life that in many settings would otherwise be disqualifying are precisely the source of his brilliance. There is something potentially patronizing about this posture if one is exaggerating the contributions one might bring in the name of being progressive or inclusive. This is not at all what we mean.

To be specific, the aforementioned Aaron and I had a series

of conversations about the psychological complexities of panhandling—the effect it has on the one asking for money, how to read those one is engaging, and more. He gets this better than anyone I have ever encountered. We talked about addictions (both of us being in recovery), and how addictions are both a cause and a perpetuator of homelessness. He brings a clarity and an understanding of these subjects that are just as valuable as even the highest-level doctoral work—if not more so. It is essential that we take the insights from the bottom seriously.

One additional note here: The novel-in-verse within this book blurs reality. Much is remembered. Some is imagined. "Aaron," and his backstory included herein, is very much real. I share it here with his permission and his blessing. I have only changed his name.

flight to egypt

(July 24th—Year One—looking back to much earlier)

Hustle is a complicated word.
A complicated world.

Freeway talked about hustlin' in "What We Do."
It's a cold winter.

Bundle up.[70]

After that first night of beat boxing,
shucking and jiving[71] for quarters,
I next saw Aaron walking
through winter in West Philly with girlfriend Ellie
and their child.

Bundle up.

Aaron
Black and slightly below average height
Always looked twenty years younger than he actually was.

Ellie
A short Irish woman
who always looked twenty years older.

One with liquor on his breath.
The other with glassy eyes and crack in her veins.

They walk their beat like a cop:
Faithful

Brave
Usually Friendly
Sometimes Dangerous.

Philly summers are blazing
Winters are what make us gritty.

Aaron and Ellie
pushed the pink stroller.
The little one rode silently
wrapped in a blanket.

Homeless child.
Away in the stroller
No crib for a bed.

"I'm sayin'
I don't mean to bother you
but can you help us get some diapers and somethin' to eat for our
    child?"

Hustle is a complicated word.
A complicated world.

They hit people up for diaper money for what seemed like weeks.
I saw them every night as I got off work
and walked to the train.

What's truth?
They needed the money.
Neither was working at the time
(hard to get a job with a criminal record—Aaron
and a middle-school degree—Ellie).
And their child needed diapers and food.

Of course they didn't need diaper money every day
but they needed the money.

Sincere eyes
a chill in the air
and the ease of compassion for a child in need...
People came out they pockets.

Hustle is a complicated word.
A complicated world.

On a particularly cold and windy December night
I saw Aaron, Ellie and their little one wrapped in a holey blanket.
They were speaking with an older woman who was a professor
    colleague of mine.

Moved by the presence
and the need for the little child
the older woman pulled some money out of her purse.
Both Aaron and Ellie reached at the same time.
No hands on the stroller.
A strong gust of wind blew over the baby's stroller.
The child fell out head first.

"Your baby!" cried the woman.

"D***! She a'ight!
Don't worry about her.
She tough! Y'nah mean?"
said Aaron, quickly moving to pick up his daughter.

But as she looked down to see if the little one was in fact alright,
the older woman noticed that the little girl wasn't crying.

She was lying still.

The woman's wrinkled face
betrayed a grief and sadness in the face of the unspeakable.
Her eyes widened, and her hands began to shake at the
    unthinkable.

Trembling and confused she turned away in shock,
but mustered the strength to look once again.

I wish we all had the courage and the nerve to look back at pain,
    and poverty, and hustle
rather than look away.

Aaron had now picked up the baby and placed her back in the
    stroller.
After taking a second look at the little one,
the old woman's face changed from a wide-eyed concern
to a squinty-eyed loathing.

It was a little plastic baby doll.

The missing right arm
wide permanent smile
and bare plastic feet gave it away.

After giving them a tongue lashing
she called the police.
Aaron got arrested
He made Ellie run away

That story has gotten a lot of mileage at cocktail parties.

I saw Aaron back on the beat a couple of months later.

Still Faithful
Brave
Friendly
and maybe Dangerous.

This time he was asking for a bus ticket.

reflections from the bottom

a theology of the bottom asks that like Christ, we not immediately recoil at the ethical complexity of those forced to hustle. How does one define "hustle"? I see this as entering into ethically complex work because "one has to do what one has to do." The Philadelphia rapper Freeway's song "What We Do" captures this "must do" spirit because—well—we do gotta feed our kids while we livin'.[72] And this theological/spiritual worldview knows that while it might not be "good," God understands. Or at the very least, God still loves us and is still with us. Praise God.

I saw this illustrated powerfully in the life of the aforementioned Aaron. I've seen him over the years partake in various hustles, including one in which he and a woman he was involved with pushed around a baby doll wrapped in a blanket. Folks couldn't see that this was just a doll and, believing that it was a real baby, were quick to offer Aaron and his partner—named "Ellie"—money. The hustle was intentionally misleading. Aaron had a criminal record and an addiction that made it difficult to find work. Ellie had a middle-school education. They did what they thought they had to do. They eventually got busted and Aaron ended up doing time.

Aaron later told me the tragic end to this episode in his life. It turned out that Aaron and Ellie were pulling the "baby doll hustle," as Aaron called it, not to (just) buy alcohol or drugs. But they did it to pay for Ellie's medication. She was HIV positive, which turned into full-blown AIDS.

Because of prior convictions, Aaron spent an extra month behind bars. While he was locked up, Ellie was on the street by herself. Something I would come to learn is that the bottom is a terrible place for anyone, but it can be especially dangerous for women who are by themselves.

Without the money from their hustle together, Ellie needed

to find a way to pay for her medications. Every time she would panhandle, without fail a man would pass by and suggestively say, "What do I get if I give you some money?"

Sex work is a complicated hustle. Don't shame folks. God is with them too.

A man assaulted her, beat her, and left her naked behind a dumpster. She didn't die from the attack. Lying outside in the rain without clothes caused her to catch pneumonia. And her weakened immune system couldn't fight any longer.

libraries and trinities

(July 25th—Year One)

One thing about life on the street,
I had a lot of time to myself.
Spent the first part of the morning
(no I didn't sleep that first night)
writing in my journal, trying to capture and expound upon
    Aaron's words.

Not a whole lot of spaces for cats on the street to go.
I'm thankful for the library.
Air-conditioning
bathroom
and a table to keep writing my notes on.

I had slipped into book-writing mode
Isolating myself,
and looking down on others because of what I knew.
Not worrying about what they thought.

I had often in my life been called "smart" or "gifted."
Test scores and conversation prove it I suppose.

(Sigh)

A Theology of the Top

I'm here sitting high in my tower
Proud
when these weren't even my ideas.
The genius here was Aaron.

I put down my pen.
Eyes staring at me
because I "look homeless"
or because I look homeless and I'm writing and reading like a
	professor in the library.

Don't close the libraries.
Not just because books need to be held
and smelled,
but because knowledge and adventure and escape reside there.
...And one can go to the bathroom with privacy and dignity
(and not have to buy something in order to use the restroom)
There is shelter from ignorance
Shelter from the elements

I left the library and walked a bit.
I would occasionally stop to write in my journal.
And then walk some more.

Hours are both slow and fast on the street.
A day of writing and walking and thinking and watching
and talking to myself and talking to no one.
Several pages and several miles.

I walk by and look deeply into the faces of others.
I see wrinkles.
Anxiety
Joy
Love and Longing
Loathing

Or I walk and notice no one.
I see no faces.
I burp and spit and pick my nose without regard to who is

watching.

When the sun started to go down on my second day, I looked for
	a safe place to sleep.
Once again a difficult decision.
Where is safe?
Where is dry?
Private enough to provide some quiet.
Public enough to provide some safety.
Out of sight so as not to be accused of loitering.
Yet within eyesight so I don't get got.

I climb over a warped metal guardrail and imagine the car that
	slid into it.
My sore legs carry me down a hill littered with patches of grass,
old food wrappers
bottles.
Ducking under the bridge I see that I am not the only one there.

Three men stand around a table
in the midst of celebrating what looked like some kind of very
	sad communion.
They gaze up at me
with red eyes swirling with both anger at being disturbed
and a longing for help.
They do not belong here.
They are not from the streets. Not like this,
But they'd been out here for a few days.

On the table was no Wine-filled Chalice or Consecrated Bread.
He was in the air close by though.

They glanced back and forth between me
and an assortment of drugs in plastic bags and bottles of liquor.

One held a pipe to his mouth.
Another had a belt pulled tight around his arm.
The other had alcohol and flame.

"He ain't no cop. Just some f****** bum."
"Who you?" another asks.

I shared and then they shared.
One of them fingered a small knife in his pocket just in case.
I kept my eye on him
just in case.

They tell me the story:

"We came to the States after giving money to some a**hole who
    promised us this
rehab program and all this other s***.
Paid money over the computer.
Paid for our ticket here.
When we arrived.
No rehab.
No job program.
Others who came had cash to get home.
We got stuck."

They have been coping in the only way they knew how.

Dulling the pain here in this hell by the river.
Beneath a bridge they don't know how to cross.

"I'm out of control man" one of them said with bloodshot crying
    eyes.
Aren't we all? I wondered silently.
Not knowing the words to say.

The quiet one, "Smokey," pulled a glass pipe to his mouth.
I say, "That stuff'll kill you man. Why you smoking that death?"

Slowly opening his eyes, Smokey answered:

"We all got our reasons.
Everybody has something different in their pipes that they are
    trying to burn up."

We stopped talking.
Didn't interview them like I interviewed Aaron.
We just sat there under the bridge.
They passed the bottle back and forth.
I didn't drink but
I d*** sure wanted to.
HALT is true, Bill![73]
I was all four.
No bottle, but I take a cigarette.

"That stuff'll kill you man,"
Smokey says back with a laugh.

With a concern for my new friends and a concern for my own
    safety
I prayed for God to be with all four of us that night.
Folded hands. Dirty and still holding a cigarette.

Amen.

Sitting on the ground
I weighed the prudence of falling asleep in this hell
I looked at the three
the glow from Smokey's lighter painting them all a soft gold.
My mouth formed a slight smile.

79

The three of them
surrounding the table
were a painful recreation of the famous icon written centuries
    ago by
Andrei Rublev.[74]

Taking out my journal I wrote and wondered if all of us are in a
    sense addicts.
What had I been addicted to?
Wealth?
Power?
Academic respect?
Maybe technology a little?
The attention that I receive?
Certainly liquor.
Lest I ever think I'm better than anybody on the bottom.

We survived the night.

The next day I went to visit the homeless outreach agency that I
    used to take my students to.
Took off my street disguise
told them about my new friends.
They helped to get the trinity into detox.[75]

reflections from the bottom

Addicts, in a sense, bear witness and reflect the rest of society. Who is the real drunk? Who is the real addict?

The scholar hymnist James Weldon Johnson wrote:

God of our weary years,
God of our silent tears,
Thou who hast brought us thus far on the way;
Thou who hast by thy might,
Led us into the light,
Keep us forever in the path, we pray.
Lest our feet stray from the places,
Our God, where we met Thee,
Lest, our hearts drunk with the wine of the world,
we forget Thee.[76]

I am in recovery. By God's grace since 1999. I drank more than anything to numb me to the pain of my life. When drunk I didn't have to think about burying parents, or broken relationships, or the strain of school or work. It's easier not having to feel.

Navigating the rough waters of reality is terrifying. It feels shaky and unsteady. We fear falling overboard. Instead of drowning ourselves, we drown the pain. We are called to show grace and love people. No matter what they are wrestling with. However, we are also called to be ferrymen carrying people and the world to sobriety on the other side.

pan

(August 16th—Year One)

"How do you ask people for money?"
My question is answered
with a stare.
Awkwardness and burnt coffee fill the air
around us at the wobbly coffee-shop table.

He started to say something...
but then he took me by the arm
led me away from the shop,
down the street
onto a bus stop bench.

"You just gon' ask me that?
How you know nuthin' 'bout the streets
and you been studying poverty all these years?"
he said appropriately scolding me.

Aaron looks away
looks back and
sighs with compassion. (He's a good teacher)

"Check it—you gotta be brave and you gotta have thick skin.
I'ma tell you like my momma use to say:

'A closed mouth never gets fed!'

So you can't just sit there expecting someone to give you
     something.
That's the craziest thing 'bout this. Rich cats be sayin' n***** like
     me is entitled and s***.

Expecting handouts.
While they kids literally get they wealth handed to them.

Nah. You gotta work, dog!
The world don't owe you a damn thing.
That's the problem with the world—we don't care about each
    other.
Ha! Don't care about each other, but we sure can get rich off each
    other ain't that right Doc?
That's what you be writing about with all your anti-capitalist stuff
    ain't it?
Well until yo' little revolution come"—
he laughs—
"everybody out here is out for they self.
So you gotta speak up if you want some help."

"OK…" I don't look up from my journal.

The teacher continues
"Listen, you approach people from afar.
You gotta read they face.
God's light shines through certain people.
That leads you to approach some
to avoid others.
Listen to they eyes.
Feel me?
Put your pen down for a minute.
God takes care of us.
That sound stupid don't it?
My girl use to always talk about how God be taking care of us and
I was like 'Then why don't He take care of me and
give a brotha a house?!'"

He paused waiting for me to laugh

but I was so enrapt by the strategy behind approaching others
that I missed the joke.

"She was right though.
He ain't never let me go to bed hungry.

And you gotta be aware of how they see you
what they think about you.
When people see me they see a Black man.
A homeless n**** and all the bulls***
that come with that.
Little white ladies see me coming and
some of them think I'm 'bout to snatch they purse.
Or if I ask a guy for some money
he think I'ma going go get drunk with it or something.
You probably thought that didn't you when you first saw me?
Nah, I'm messing wit you.
Put it this way
you need to be aware of yoself AND aware of who they are.
So I overcompensate.
Move slowly
hands out.
Speak from far away.
Not too loud
but they have to hear you.
Smile
but not too much.
Look too happy,
then you don't look like you need anything.
Look too sad,
you'll depress somebody and they'll resent you for that.
Don't chase anyone
Got arrested for that once
That's why I can't go on your campus no more...

And, this is messed up but you gon' have to take off that
watch
Gotta look homeless, but not too homeless.
It's like folks don't want you to have nothing nice.
I can't answer this"—he says pulling out a phone—
"when I'm working."

I noted that he called it working.
And I noted that he had a cell phone.
Why surprised?

"I need a phone," Aaron continues.
"When I apply to jobs they have to have a way to get in touch
     with me.
My sister calls to make sure I'm still alive.
It's a pay-as-you-go plan.
Works for me.
I got a bike too.
But folks at the coffee shop
and downtown where I go around eleven won't know about that."

"Thanks man," I said.
"I really appreciate it."

"Don't appreciate it.
Do something about it.
Shouldn't nobody have to be out here beggin'.
Do something!
Do something crazy!" he said with a laugh, taking his leave and
     going back
to work.

reflections from the bottom

The "contorting" that many people of color feel the need to do when under the white gaze is both exhausting and tragic. Modulating and slowing down in response to potential white anxiety is a learned behavior—one that disallows the true self to walk and fly freely.

How much more the contorting that someone asking for money must do. In this case it is not just symbolic or professional survival at stake, but perhaps literal survival. The judging gaze from the housed and successful is cruel. What's worse: the cruelty of that gaze or the not being seen at all?

Thus, the work of a theology of the bottom must be seeing with God's eyes. More than just adding glasses, we need to replace our eyes with God's eyes—eyes that see and love the true self, allowing the other to be however and whoever they truly are.

I love when elders reply to "It's good to see you!" with "It's good to be seen!"

It is, isn't it?

plague—frogs

(April 1st—Year Two)

Nineteen Eighties
Funding for mental health facilities in our nation—
drastically cut
resulting in closures.
Where do the former residents go
but the streets?

I wonder as I wander:[77]
Does the street drive people to madness
or does madness drive and chain people to the street?

The burning bush would say:
"It is a mad society
that drives people to and leaves people
on the street."

This plague was for her.

More and more
we were feeling that
art
spoke so clearly to our struggle
capturing what mere words could not.
We had employed visual art already.
Now we strike through theater.

As was the case with our first plagues
I cannot take credit for its origins.
The Hebrews pointed to *Ha-Shem*[78]

87

I too point to God working through my old university colleagues
and the subject matter of a course that they co-taught.
The course explored
Augusto Boal's
Theater of the Oppressed[79]—
a powerful intersection between theatrics and the struggle for
    liberation.

Theater of the Oppressed?
A group of thinly rehearsed actors
a left-leaning play
a public space
a transient group
of mostly disinterested spectators?
Yes and...[80]
Far more than that.
One of Boal's great emphases:
"We are all actors."
And when the
Theater of the Oppressed
is in action
there are actors and spect-actors
not spectators
with all present playing a role.

The benches and our Yeshiva Without Walls
were transformed into an actors' studio.
The preparations for this
production
were especially painful for those of us
previously
diagnosed with mental disabilities.
I don't like that word "disability."
I do like when people say

"differently abled."

One brother told the painful story
of being called a "r****d"
after his untreated bipolar disorder
began to affect his behavior in severe ways during high school.
His wet eyes betrayed a pain
all who have been the target of hateful slurs could understand.

We knew what we were going to do
we just did not know when or where.
Public demonstrations and prophetic acts:
As much about their context as they are their content.
There is always a message in the context.

We chose one of the strangest
"craziest"
traditions held by our city.

April Fool's Day
our city holds what they call
The Spring Mummers Parade.
Difficult to describe
but it is essentially a series of brief
musical
costumed
choreographed
performances prepared by "mummers clubs"
celebrating a more than three-hundred-year-old tradition.

As the story goes
the diverse group of individuals described as Swedes
brought many "old world" traditions
along with them to the

colonies,
one of which was the tradition of spending New Year's Day
going from house to house in costume
entertaining those who dared answer the door.
These individuals became known as shooters
(for the loud noise made by their guns!) and
mummers. They were rewarded with food and drink.
That tradition has grown into a full parade
sans firearms
with clubs competing before judges
dancing before crowds
and enduring the consistently chilly winter weather on New Year's
    Day as well as
the unpredictability of April 1st.

This eccentric local tradition was just crazy enough for us to
disturb.

Security was of course suspicious when Aaron and I showed up
to sit in the large audience.
Cops kept a close eye on our every move.
After our last artistic activities
they had a right to be suspicious.
To be clear, they are not the villains in this story.
They were just doing their job.
We tryna free them too.

Midway through the parade
Aaron and I began to invite attention.
We reached into our bags and pretended to be looking for
    something.
Praying as we rummaged.
We pulled a large stack of flyers out
and proceeded to distribute them to anyone

who'd take these little pieces of green paper.
They read:
"We are not the crazy ones.
A City and Nation that doesn't care about the homeless is crazy."
And on the back it said
"Your shame not ours."

Officers stopped us.
"Yooze guys got a permit to distribute here at the parade?"
Didn't matter.
We were just the distraction.

Misdirection

As they began to escort us away,
nineteen "actors"
slid out from beneath the VIP viewing stand
where they had been hiding since before sunrise.
Dressed in all green clothing they began to
jump up and down and
roll around the street shouting
"Homelessness is crazy. Not us!"

Another actress in all green who was sitting among the spectators
began to scream:
"What's crazy is that I haven't eaten in three days!"

A man in green fatigues sitting elsewhere yelled:
"What's crazy is that I served this country overseas and now I am
    sleeping on the street!"

Actor after actor
placed randomly in different seats in the audience began yelling
    rehearsed lines

and then holding up a sign with their words written in green
(so that the network cameras and handheld phone cameras could
    capture the messages as well).
More than fifty of us in total participated.
And it was all caught on television
until the producers of the show cut away.

Television producers are told that they should
never give disrupting activists a microphone.
So they cut to the commentators who acted as if nothing had
    happened.
We anticipated that.

They could ignore a group of loud homeless activists,
but they could not ignore one of the parade's participants.

The next float coming in front of the
VIP
platform was the Crazy Frogs Comics Brigade.
This Mummers Club had been known to
push the envelope before with their politically charged floats.
They never won the competition,
but they were always among the most memorable of the clubs.
The president of the Crazy Frogs was actually the
one who came down and bailed us out of jail
after the art installation plague.
He was so moved by what we were trying to do
(his parish was one of the churches that placed the church
    sculptures on their altar)
that he had been coming to the benches regularly.
He brought the idea of participating in the second plague to his
    leadership board
and by some miracle they kept it a secret.
The cameras and producers could ignore us, but they could not

ignore one of the parade's participating clubs.

A large float was pushed in.

The company constructed a large green house atop of a moving
    flatbed.
On the outside
of the painted wooden structure was written
"Frog Asylum."

Each club has two minutes to fill with a routine
that they have usually rehearsed for months.
Theirs (ours) was written just three weeks ago
replacing what they were previously working on.

The two minutes began with a man acting as
The President of the United States
speaking while surrounded by secret servicemen.
The actor stands up, says
(lip-synching previously recorded lines)
"I hereby close all government-run mental health facilities.
Go on—you're on your own now.
There's plenty of benches and heat vents for you to sleep on."[81]

After the president stopped speaking
the doors of the Frog Asylum slowly opened.
The Frog orchestra who were walking behind the float began to
    play
recording artist Janelle Monáe's song "War of the Roses."[82]

This is when we come alive!

As the song played,
dozens of us wearing green straitjackets walked through the door

where the
"secret servicemen"
undid their restraints.
When free, the "formerly institutionalized men" revealed shirts
    that said,
"Let's do something crazy!"
Their choreography was chaotically powerful.
They
danced and danced
and got
closer and closer
to the barriers that were set up on the side of the streets to keep
    spectators to the side.
As the song drew to a close (and mind you no one was cheering)
the dancers leapt over the barriers and kept dancing in the
    crowd.
By this point the next float had already begun their routine,
but that did not stop the frogs from overtaking the audience.
Through screaming and disgust
they made their way up to the VIP platform where the
mayor and other dignitaries were sitting.
Security only got a few of them,
but several others climbed over chairs
sat on the laps of the mayor and his entourage.
They kept dancing on and around the mayor chanting:
"Free the homeless!
clap-clap-clap, clap, clap
Free the homeless!
clap-clap-clap, clap, clap
Free the homeless!"
The leader of the Crazy Frogs
taped a green piece of paper with a list of demands to the
    mayor's bald head and
whispered to him,

"Do something crazy and try to end chronic homelessness in the
  city Mr. Mayor."
He was tackled and thrown in the back of the wagon with the rest
  of us.

reflections from the bottom

What role should madness play in liberation? By connotation, the word "madness" evokes something negative and abnormal. We mean not that. Nor do we mean to minimize the challenges of navigating life while being differently abled mentally. What we mean by madness is being wired in a way that is not the norm—not bad—just not the norm. Or in regard to societal change, being "mad" enough to see and then work for something very different than the current order. Vision like that is so unusual and disturbing that it is often called "crazy" or "mad." So be it.

Like many aspects of life on the streets, I risk romanticizing or understating the devastation certain mental conditions can have on a life. It is not my intent to simply use something so serious and difficult as just a literary tool to tell a story. I have a relative to whom I am very close who later in life was diagnosed with schizophrenia. It has hurt so much seeing the challenges she has had to navigate in her relationships, her workplace, and in how she sees herself. She is both brilliant and burdened. Some moments "like she used to be" and other moments like someone I hardly know.

The journey for me has been one of grieving, feeling helpless, having to get over the stigma, remembering that she is far more than her diagnosis, to landing in a place of hope and loving again. To me, she is in a way unhoused. I do my best to bring home to her.

sade

(September 9th—Year One)

I had survived two months on the street,
but I needed a bit of a break—
a break not only from the wear of sleeping outside,
but also from walking.

My feet needed a rest
so they took me to the train station.
Many of the women and men
particularly those who are described as chronically homeless
(as opposed to those who are temporarily without residence)
know that the train station is a gift towards their survival
especially in the winter time.

There is a constant stream of announcements in the background
    there.
It's fine
I had been sleeping with the sounds of outdoors life.

No good sleep on the streets.

Finding an open space between two people waiting for a train
I sit down with beard and baggage
and take out my journal.
The woman to my left coughed and tried to hide the fact
that she was holding her breath as she grabbed her bag and left.

I wonder
do I care or not?

I pulled out my pen and picked up where I had left off yesterday.

While writing, I grew hungry.
I guess I'll do what so many others do every day in order to
    survive.

I wonder
do I feel shame or not?

I would experience another aspect of being on the bottom.
I'd beg.
Can't be so hard.
Until then I had survived on the box of protein bars I brought in
    my backpack.

I was strangely excited.
I was really doing it!
(On reflection I am embarrassed by my thrill at doing something
    that so many are forced to do simply to make it from day to
    day.)
The excitement wore off quickly however,
once I had packed up my bag and stood up with the intent of
    really doing it.

I try to remember what Aaron taught me.

Mustering up the courage
to ask a complete stranger for money...
so much harder than it looks.

The first challenge is in figuring out what to say.
I tried out a number of variations in my mind.

"Can you spare some change?"

No too informal.
"Would you please help me get something to eat?"
Felt a little too sad and depressing.
"Excuse me Sir…"

I considered coming up with a story.
Some kind of a hustle.
Something that might move them to give.
Should I smile?
Or look sad?
Aaron's words were swimming in my head.
I was overthinking this.

I wondered who to ask first.
Some people "didn't look like they had money to spare"
so I didn't ask them.
Others didn't look nice enough.

Identifying a kind-faced man wearing a suit, but no tie,
I braced myself in the ten seconds before the man would cross my
    path,
all the while trying to dismiss the fact that I was really about to
    "beg for money."
I was hungry.
But all of this was for research purposes anyway, right?

"Excuse me Sir…" He passed by without letting me get the words
    out.

"Sir, excuse me…" Another incomplete sentence.

The only response I got was,
"Sorry pal, not today."
"I don't have anything on me."

"Sorry I don't carry cash on me."

Person after person after person
after person.
I counted.
I asked twenty-two people.
Not one stopped. Not one shared.
I could hear the change in their pockets. Each had purses or
    wallets.
I was steps from an ATM.
Person after person after person
after person.

Aaron was right you do have to have thick skin for this.

The cold, dismissive looks on their faces began to get to me.

"Excuse me Ma'am, can you help me get something to eat?"
Without looking at me, a woman seemingly on her way to work
dropped a quarter into my extended hand
    careful not to make contact.

The singer Sade's haunting verse came to mind.

She didn't want to touch my hand. Too much.[83]

Who can understand the strength of character
—or is it desperation—
that one must have in order to beg and panhandle.
Scratching my head, I realized how unkempt I must have looked.
And I'd gone a few weeks without shaving.
Washing up in a restroom, one can only do so much.

After the thirtieth person had gone by

I no longer needed money as much as
I wanted someone to just look me in the eye
let me speak
ask my name
and let me be human.

I started to speak louder.

"Excuse me Miss! Can you help me get some..."
She walked away.
I took a few steps after her.
"Excuse me! Can you help me get..."
She walked faster.
With the smell of food
coming from the restaurants in the train station only intensifying
my hunger
I started to run after her.

"Please can you help me? Stop ignoring me!"
I was nearly yelling when a police officer grabbed me harder than
    I had been grabbed in a long time.

"Hey buddy" said the cop,
"Get out of here. Don't harass these people."

"No no I'm not really home—" I caught myself.

I had been stopped before,
unfairly racially profiled really,
when walking to my office late one night wearing jeans and a
    hooded sweatshirt.
When I told that officer that I was a professor, the situation
    completely changed.
That cop got transferred three weeks later.

I kept my other life a secret in this situation though.
The officer continued.

"If I catch you again, I'll take you in for aggressive panhandling.
Three hundred dollar fine or a week in jail.[84]
Get lost."

I picked up my bag and walked away shocked and angry.
"Hey!" the officer called after me.
"The Cathedral has a soup kitchen after the midday service.
Lot of folks get lunch there."

Resentment, gratitude, shame, anger,
and sadness
all swirled around in my mind.
A few steps away from the train station, I took out my journal and
    tried to write, but couldn't.
The man who in a very different season of life had published four
    books
couldn't write a single word now.
My hands just shook.
Pen in my right
twenty-five cents in the left.

reflections from the bottom

The ethics of undercover ethnographic research is debated in sociology programs around the US. The scholar assumes and performs an identity with the goal of a deep enough acceptance to be received by a community and then learn about a culture/ space/group from the inside.

Even as I write this, I still feel a tension within about "pretending to be homeless." And yet, I gently extend an invitation to you, dear friend, to do the same.

Go down to learn. Go down in solidarity. Go down for the spiritual pilgrimage that it is. Go down for freedom. You will not return the same. It's terrible.

And while down there—down here—be anonymous. Don't let folks know it's you. Don't do this for any glory or admiration. Just be with. And beg. And then give away whatever you get. At least look someone in the eye. Give them the dignity of being treated like a human. And if you can, talk. And listen. And Love.

Be free. Be safe. Be brave.

luther was right

(September 9th—Year One)

Stunned and hungry I walked into the cathedral.
Perhaps that is how we should always enter into religious spaces.
I saw a priest
a woman
celebrating communion in the surprisingly bright sanctuary.
I sat down in an old but not uncomfortable pew with another
    man
towards the back of the church.
He got up and moved to another pew because of, presumably, my
    smell.

I hadn't been on the street long enough to stop caring about how
    mean people can be.

Fists balled
teeth clenched,
I walked towards the front of the church to receive.

I kneeled down at the altar and extended my dirty hands,
just as I did every Sunday at my congregation near the university.

When the priest came to me,
she graciously did not react to my smell,
or my unshaved face,
or even the slow tears streaming down my face.

She placed a piece of bread in my hands saying,
"The Body of Christ. The Bread of Heaven."
Quickly the deacon followed saying in a barely audible mumble,

"The Blood of Christ. The Cup of Salvation."

I ate and I drank
It was a feast to me.
For stomach and for heart.

"The Bread of Heaven."

They returned to the altar
the congregation returned to their seats.
Everyone except me.
I remained kneeling at the altar,
hands still extended.
I stayed there frozen,
through the closing prayer and the recessional hymn.
Unsure why, I didn't move.
I just stared at my hands.

After the sanctuary was empty,
the priest returned and
invited me to the meal in the building next door. I was quiet.

"Excuse me Sir" she said. "Would you like to get something to
    eat?"

reflections from the bottom

Luther was right.

"*Wir sind Bettler. Hoc est verum.*"[85]

An important mark of a theology of the bottom is the recognition of the humanity of individuals. The great journalist and author, James Spady, is known to say that "we are all in process," alluding to the fact that not only is no one perfect, but that we are all on a journey of improvement and growth.

This allows us to see with grace-filled, prophetic eyes—not only what one is, but also what one might someday become. This is never giving up on anyone, recognizing that no one is beyond redemption.

Thus, we seek to not see the world through good and evil lenses. This is not a denial of the existence of evil; rather it is believing that evil is something that is done by people. People are not bad; they just sometimes do bad things. And all bad things have a source—soil from which they emerge.

As a seminarian, I met a young poet named Anne Marie who once penned in a poetic letter she shared with me: "Fear is the garden of sin."[86] Over time, to that I've come to add "hurt" as well, for the wounded heart is often a source of great compassion or great violence.

Knowledge that those around us who are doing wrong do so for a reason should allow us to see and appreciate their humanity and their potential to be redeemed.

It's radical to believe in the potential for redemption. A person who robs stores and/or deals drugs is not an evil person. Perhaps it was life circumstances, mental health, fear, a lack of options, a lack of education that led them to this point in their lives. Hopelessness, desperation, and the feeling of being dehumanized can take an individual to depths that they did not know they possessed.

The humility and strength of character that one must feel in order to bring oneself to panhandle or beg for money or for food is something deeply foreign to most of us. If it were not hard enough to have to extend your hand and beg for scraps, the experience of being ignored by people who have the means to change your life is heartbreaking. And those who stop often give you only a few coins, never touching your hand, never looking you in the eyes, never asking your name. Over time, for some this is just too much. Their voice gets louder. They throw away politeness and no longer care about how they look. And the hurt of dehumanization and the fear of starving soon bears a bitter fruit.

Ahhh, now that the beggar is "loud and aggressive" we at last see him or her—only long enough to remove them from the previously peaceful space.

a theology of the bottom can understand what the street can do to a person. Not in a patronizing sense, but in a humanizing one, recognizing that all of us are in process. All of us are beggars with hands extended, though we may reach for different things. The great reformer Martin Luther's final written words speak to this.

"Wir sind Bettler. Hoc est verum."

"We are all beggars—this is true."

plague—locusts

(May 1st—Year Two)

Our numbers began to grow.
And after each of our attempts at raising awareness about
    homelessness
(the media first called these plagues, not us),
we were under much greater scrutiny.
That's the challenging thing about campaigns like this.
You want more attention for the cause
not for the actors.
More eyes made pulling off any more demonstrations or plagues
    very difficult.
Good thing the third plague was not planned by us,
but rather by the city's ministerial alliance.

After the art plagues and
after the madness parade,
several local clergy members began spending
more time on the street and
more time with us.
What they saw and heard became the subject matter of an
    interfaith council meeting.
After a conversation about "what they could do to help"
one of the older ministers present asked if anyone there had
    heard of a woman named
Debbie Little
or the ministry she founded in Boston.

She told them the story of Debbie Little and "Common
    Cathedral."[87]
This is an outdoor street church

that gathers near the fountain in Boston Commons rain or shine
   (or snow).
The street church was comprised of mostly individuals
   experiencing
homelessness
though other congregations, often from the suburbs, would
worship with them and provide lunch afterwards.
The ministry also provided free legal counsel, pastoral support for
   those who were
ill,
an arts ministry, and advocacy as well.

Yet, it's more than just a church gathering.
Their very presence is a prophetic act.
Homeless women and men standing together outside,
gathering in the name of God
stories below billion-dollar business offices.

The idea of this street church caught on.
Eventually there were street churches in nearly every major city
   in the US
and dozens of street congregations around the world.
In Philly they are called the Welcome Church.[88]

When the minister shared this story,
the group began to envision what the third plague might look like.
Unlike the previous two efforts, for this one
we simply went along for the ride.

Rittenhouse Square,
a park in our city,
dates back to colonial times.
It's one of the original five city parks
planned by William Penn and Thomas Holme.[89]

These were meant to be common spaces
where different types of people could come together and share
    space
as equals.
It is a beautiful albeit small four-square blocks,
green space
filled with benches and small paths all leading to a large fountain
that flows for about four months of the year.
During the week, it is a common outside lunch space
for those who work in the surrounding buildings,
stay-at-home parents
and nannies who wish to bring little ones and pets outside for a
    walk.
Unlike other parks downtown,
one rarely sees any of us sleeping on benches in Rittenhouse.
We are forced to "keep moving" because of the oddly stringent
no-loitering laws.
So individuals who "look" homeless only pass through
occasionally asking for change,
while those who don't look homeless may loiter as long as they
    like.

Around the park's edges are high-end apartment and office
    buildings.
On their ground floors are several of the city's most popular
    restaurants
each of which seems to be led by a celebrity chef
and frequented by those who wish to be seen
and those who can afford the pricy dishes.

The one business on the square that those of us on the street
    ever saw the inside of
was the two-story bookstore at the corner.
It had one of the few public restrooms

and un-harassing respites from extreme heat and deadly cold
    close by.

On this bright Sunday in May,
it was a comfortable 60 degrees
The park saw a number of dog walkers, joggers, and non-church-
    going shoppers
walking through the park.
In the neighborhood around the square
there are ten religious congregations within three blocks in every
    direction.
The participating houses of worship each
very subtly changed their worship times for that day to twelve
    noon.
The two synagogues and a local mosque all invited their members
    to Sunday lunches.
The lunches and the worship services all were
"coincidentally"
scheduled to take place outside in the park.

They billed it as an interfaith day of worship in the square.
The local papers and news stations all deemed it
worthy enough to send reporters and cameras...

The separate services and gatherings began in proximity to one
    another
yet out of earshot.
"Oh how good and how pleasant it is..."[90]
Fifteen minutes into their time,
the Imam
the Priests
the Rabbis
the Pastors made eye contact.
We sat on the side of the park in front of the bookstore watching.

111

People underestimate how much people on the streets see.
The officer watching us was too late to perceive the clerical plans
	in action.

The worshippers moved.
Mostly middle-aged
Silver Foxes and White-Haired Queens walked towards the
	restaurants.
Then the civilized suburbanites
of these commuter congregations began to erase social norms.
Finally.

No one saw it as crazy that
a few humans would spend
a few hundred dollars
in a world-class restaurant on food
while just outside the window other humans were starving.
But we've gotten used to this.
We've stopped noticing.

Not this crew.
Not this plague.
They walked right into the four restaurants and
began picking up the plates of stunned couples
just trying to enjoy Sunday brunch.
And after they took the plates,
they walked outside and brought them over to us.

Motherf****** Robin Hood.
You d*** right we ate that five-star food. With pleasure.

The police came quickly
as this would be a financial blow to the culinary destinations of
	the city.

They arrested several of the demonstrators and
of course they arrested us.
The law students that were volunteering helped us get released
    quickly.
Better than Torts class huh?

Before the night was over they hit nearly twenty other
    restaurants.

The most beautiful part of the evening to me
was how those who had not been taken
to the precinct returned to the square and began to sing together.

And they sang well into the night.

The fifth plague.

reflections from the bottom

An early twentieth-century Chicago-based author and humorist named Finley Peter Dunne wrote a syndicated column featuring the fictional voice of a character named "Mr. Dooley." Dooley — an Irish immigrant bartender — spoke a quote that would also be uttered by the great theologians Reinhold Niebuhr and Martin Marty, though in a different context.[91] The character, Dooley, said that newspapers were to "comfort the afflicted and afflict the comfortable." The later theologians would apply this same quote to the work of Christians and all activists living in the world today.

There is a truth in this that is of great import to the work of a theology of the bottom. Both for the academic/journalistic work of this theology as well as for the applied activist side. Afflicting the comfortable can be — admittedly — uncomfortable. But if the cause is urgent enough...

code blue

(November 1st—Year One)

I got nothing.
Nothing I got.

Life can be so cold sometimes.
In this city they call it
Code Blue.
Emergency speak
for a dangerous
deadly freeze.
Police keep an extra eye out for folks
on the street.
Shelters add extra beds for the expectation
that the hard-core guys
will come in for a night or two.
And hopefully the coffee shops and bookstores
Will be a little more
chill
about moving people back out
into the cold.

You wanna know why cats on the street
talk to themselves?
Go for a three-hour walk
in 30-degree weather.

Is it pride or fear
that keeps me out here
and not in a shelter?

Proud of being younger
and hard core?
Fear of someone taking my s***
when I'm asleep in there?
My need to be alone?
Fear of being known?

AA Meeting brought an hour of warmth and a cup of coffee this
    morning.
We ride trains to survive the rest of the day.

Begged quarters and dimes.
Enough to push through the turnstile
and ride up and down
the blue line.

Ya know Billie Holiday
lived here.[92]

"Southern trees bear strange fruit."[93]
And northern streets hold
fallen fruit that will die and rot
if not picked up soon.

Code Blue

I ride this train back and forth.
I sit in the way back.
Rosa I'm sorry.

And I see the wrinkled-up noses
and the shaking heads.
I see you leaving this car
because the smell—

my smell—
is unbearable to you.

And I sit on a knife's edge
deciding whether I care or not.

Does embarrassment outweigh
my need for warmth and rest?

Where would you have me shower?

I got nothing.
Nothing I got.

A redheaded twenty-something
walks up and down this blue line.

"Good evening ladies and gentlemen
My name is Joseph. I got laid off earlier this year
I've been homeless the last six weeks
and haven't been able to find work.
I'm hungry and if you have anything to spare
it would mean a lot."

Crickets.

Until someone stands up and hands him a banana.

"Thank you so much."

And then a dollar from a nurse on her way in to the night shift.

"Thank you so much."

Joseph crosses into another car
and I keep riding until I'm kicked off.

I'll sleep in the train station until the sun comes up.

reflections from the bottom

Public nuisance is a complicated aspect of our society often dictated by location and a variance in cultural norms. We wrestle with the questions: How shall we respond to the interruption to our peaceful commute or walk through the city? What do we do with the smell? What does compassion, patience, and love without being patronizing or belittling look like? And yet should we become a public nuisance as well to help those on the street?

When did we become so proficient at ignoring suffering? What numbed us—broke us—getting us to the point where we can glance and then quickly forget someone who is hungry or without shelter. Children passing someone on the street are stunned and look to their adults for explanation or compassionate response. Sometimes we explain, sometimes we share a bit with someone begging, sometimes we get into protection mode. Maybe we should instead listen to the little teachers at our side.

302

(November 9th—Year One)

50 said I should go 'head and switch the style up.
Of course they'll hate but watch this money pile up.[94]

Beggin' on the train and over in the north part of town
I got nothing
nothing I got.
So I decided to change it up a bit.
Can't move in on someone's turf if they were already working a
    corner,
so I sought out an unoccupied space.
I landed on a heavily trafficked sidewalk
near a large fountain near the beginning of the parkway
leading to the city's museum district.
High-end hotels
Straight Cash Homie.[95]

"Excuse me Sir, can you help the homeless?"
I began with a little more confidence in my voice.
"Sir? Could you please spare some change to help me get
    something to eat?"
Nothing.
Nothing again.

A group of school children walking to the science center passed
    me and
their teacher says "Stay close! Remember we don't talk to
    strangers."
Thanks.

"Um, please, no loitering in front of the hotel.
I told you this last week. Do I have to call the police again?"
I heard a redcap from the hotel say.

"Uh...sorry." I moved away confused
but realizing that he had gotten me mixed up with someone else.
Had I not been so hungry, I would have laughed at how he
    "thought we all looked the same."
Gentle micro-aggressions.

"Hello Miss? Miss? I'm sorry to bother you, but could you spare
    something to help me get some food? Please I..."
"I'm so sorry I don't carry cash on me. Sorry,"
the fast-walking twenty-something said.
"Alright, God bless you," I replied.

I just stopped asking for a little while.
I sat on a bench and reconsidered my approach.
I noticed that I wasn't the only street person in the area.

She was maybe in her forties—
walking and talking to herself. Yelling.

Replaying conversations from years ago? Days ago? Never ago?
No, the old pain, anger and fear
was too real in this replay for this to be made up.
Still fresh.

She seemed to see her interlocutor
in the face of anyone who dared make eye contact with her.

I saw someone pull out their phone and dial a number as the
    yelling sister was now walking in the street into traffic.

A few minutes later
a few cops later
many angry drivers later
the situation began to escalate

A small crowd
staring
pointing
horns still blaring.

In this city, what was about to happen is called a "302."
It's the legal classification for an involuntary commitment to a
    mental facility
It is one of the worst things that anyone can witness.

A 302 can only be issued if someone is a danger to others or a
    danger to themselves.

"Ma'am, we're gonna need you to come with us."
"Don't touch me!
I won't let another man hit me!
You stay the hell away.
Y'all didn't do s*** when I called sayin' he was beating my a**
    back then.
Now you here.
F*** YOU!
Don't TOUCH me!"—
she breathes heavy
eyes darting looking for safety—
"I'm not crazy!
This city is crazy!
F*** YOU!"
"Ma'am, this is your final warning.
Come with us or we will have to use force," the other officer said.

It all happened so quickly.
One approached from the front.
The other snuck up from behind and wrapping his arms around
    her,
lifted her off of the ground.

"Nooooo!
I'm not crazy!
Noooooo!"

They tried to 'cuff her
one of her arms got free
she struck a young-looking officer across the face.
He didn't hesitate in using his taser on her.
Her scream was shrill but sad.
Her body went limp and was soon carried into the back of the
    police cruiser which spirited her away to a downtown Mental
    Health Facility.

And then everyone went about their business.

Me too.

"Got some money for the homeless Miss?"

reflections from the bottom

There is a temptation to romanticize the intersection between madness and genius. The "fine line" between the two is almost lauded in film and literature and in our recollections of historic brilliance. The trope of the "Mad Scientist" or the "Brilliant But Evil Dictator" is always fascinating, but never complete.

On the other hand, there is the great stigma that often accompanies "mental illness." Individuals can be dismissed and thought of as "less than" in ways that hinder their careers, hire-ability, perceptions in school, and relationships.

a theology of the bottom does its best to withhold judgement, knowing that there are individuals struggling both inside the mansion and on the streets *and* that there is brilliance both in the boardroom and on the benches. Further, we know that humans are complex in their ability to not only hold multiple emotions in one moment, but to also hold brilliance and fogginess simultaneously.

a picture of the future

(November 17th—Year One)

"I drew this picture of you.
Can I get like five for it?"

This was her hustle.
How she ate.

I got to know her a little bit while waiting in line at one of the
     food distributions
that some church did on Saturday mornings.

She calls herself Destiny.
Not an addict.
Not "crazy."
She got put out of her house.

Trans.

Back in the day, cats on the streets used to be called "Transy"
short for transient.
A sign of instability.
On the move from place to place
looking for work or a place to lay our heads.

This is a different kind of transient.
Maybe the same.
The lack of housing stability that
too many queer youth have after coming out.[96]

Destiny's out here

tryna paint a picture of what life can be.
Was dangerous at home and in school
so she hit the streets.
You hear that?
Life was so dangerous that she thought street life was safer.

This isn't a theological question about what God thinks about
    being queer or trans.
The question is how is Destiny gonna eat?
Will someone kill Destiny?

You know what she does when she's not drawing someone?
Reads the Bible.

That she was painting pictures outside of the Art Museum wasn't
    lost on her.
"I'm like a little Da Vinci.
Left-handed.
Queer.
Artist.
Why the hell not?
He's the past,
I'm the future.
And if my family can't see that...
well, that's a them problem."

Destiny died three weeks after I met her.
She was lit on fire by a bunch of teenagers.

reflections from the bottom

Does the theological and ecclesial wrestling of the church and of church policy-makers matter on the street? This isn't meant to suggest that theology and polity are done in vain. We glorify God with our minds through these pursuits. Yet, out here we wrestle with life and death, "powers and principalities."[97] Thus questions like "Should LGBTQ individuals be ordained?" are dismissed for more pressing ones like "Since I was kicked out of my home for being a lesbian, where will I eat and sleep tonight?"

There is no question of "hating the sin and loving the sinner." We seek to celebrate "being with" over "being right."

One further note—and this is complicated—one does not need to agree theologically or politically with others in these unhoused spaces. Homelessness doesn't discriminate between those it carries down to the street. Shelters have a lot of different people on their cots. We don't need to agree politically or theologically to lock arms down here. I'll meet you there. The poet, God-lover, and religious leader Rumi writes of us meeting "out beyond ideas of wrongdoing and rightdoing."[98] Ameen.

plague—distance

(June 7th—Year Two)

"There are, perhaps, two types of poets,"
I remembered my colleague from the English department saying
    some years ago.

"Those who write by candlelight hidden in their homes and
those who write by sunlight outside.
They both have sources of light by which to write,
yet one melts away never to return while
the other always comes back after disappearing."

Under one gray afternoon sky
my daily walkabout took me by the river that ran through the
    middle of the city.
There I met a poet of the latter breed.

I sat down not far from him
so as to put down a few ideas that had come while I was walking.
He saw me writing in my journal when he suddenly asked
with an innocent awkwardness, "Are you a poet?"

I so very much wanted to say yes, but I replied,
"I want to be...I'm working on a book about God and life out here
    on the streets—life on the bottom."

The poet was well kempt,
but the large trash bag full of clothes and other things
made me think that they too were swimming through
    homelessness,
though I'd never seen this person out here before.

128

I asked what he was working on
A smile and then he said that he was trying to prove that
art can change the world.

He's been writing poems and leaving them around the city
hoping that someone will pick them up and read what they have
    to say.

A brilliant idea.
A gentle act of change
(plague)

This day the poet was working on a poem called "Distance."
And from there a most remarkable conversation ensued.

"Distance" the poet began, not reading the poem but saying what
    was in between the lines,
"is one of the great teachers.
What happens in the distance is a longing—a heightened
    awareness.
God is in the distance"

The two of us sat silently for minutes that seemed like restful
    days.

"Have you ever had to leave someone or something you loved?
And then that feeling, that longing in your chest...
God the Creator is at work in that space,
that distance between you and the beloved."

Stillness and years passed by.

"I've come quite a distance, from where I began," I added.
"And it's made me more aware of the distance between people.

The rich and the poor
The top and the bottom."

"Maybe words can make up the distance" the poet replied.
"I'm trying to encourage others to write poems and leave them
    around like I've been doing.
I don't sign them.
These poems are free
like words
like I am
like we all should be."

The Order of Anonymous Beggars
for one night became the order of anonymous poets.
We wrote one poem for everyone on the street and in the shelter
    system.
Thousands.
Some good
Some powerful
Some that didn't make any sense.

This wasn't our greenest plague
It was certainly our most quiet.

We're just trying to make up the distance.

reflections from the bottom

The bottom, homelessness, and the human experience are—
or I should say could be—like poetry. "No one buys poetry,"
a publisher once told me. There are some who faithfully read
and write it, but they are in the minority. It's the literary genres
that make money that get the most attention from agents and
publishing houses.

And while often overlooked, poetry is free. Mary Oliver,
Rumi, Sonia Sanchez, Pablo Neruda, Mirabai, Kabir, Matsuo
Basho. Free. All dem.

I first learned this concept of liberated writing though, from
not a poet, but rather a journalist named James Spady. Find his
articles and find his books. He writes from the promised land.
Never changing his words for an editor's prerogative. He writes
like we speak—breaking grammatical rules when a sentence or
a story calls for it. He writes what he wants, when he wants, and
how he wants.

a theology of the bottom must be free in its writing, teaching,
and application. How can a theological field work for liberation
when it is not liberated itself? Thus what does liberation for a
theologian look like?

It is not being beholden to the tenure and promotional process.
This tempts scholars to hold their tongues (or writing) for fear
of offending those who will "decide their academic futures." It
leads individuals to write and teach that which they hope will be
accepted and popular, rather than the hard truths.

Being free theologically is not just writing to the academic
audience (as we are taught to do), but instead writing in an
accessible way. This is not "dumbing one's writing down." This
is considering a broader audience.

And yet I don't romanticize this freedom. Free scholars are
often overlooked, stepped over, even hated. As some overlook,

step over, and hate poetry. As some overlook, step over, and hate folks on the street.

What's free? This charge to be free is not exclusively for theologians or poets, but for all of us. New Hampshire is known for its motto, "Live Free or Die." This revolutionary refrain might be interpreted inversely: We are most alive when we are free! And "Where the Spirit of the Lord is, there is freedom."[99] Come, Holy Spirit!

shelters

(November 23rd—Year One)

I sample Sia on loop. Let's be clear. I trust no one.[100]

I'm not sure I totally trust myself in here.

The cold was too bitter.
Street outreach
asked me if I wanted to come in.
MSW with a good heart and bad pay
made a call and found a bed for me.

Now I'm on a cot
not-sleeping
next to 300 of my brothers.
Down here on the bottom.

And I complain about the food
about the lack of privacy
about the intake worker with the bad attitude
But I'm grateful.
I won't freeze tonight because of this place.

But let's be clear, I trust no one.
I'm not sure I totally trust myself in here.

Cot next to me?
He's asleep.
Bag open...
Gloves.

Hat.
Subway pass.

I sit up.
He wakes up
with the survival-driven sixth sense one develops from
sleeping in public.

Let's be clear...

A bladder full of burned coffee and the desire to piss indoors
Lifts me off the cot.
I bring all my stuff.

Let's be clear...

And I wait.

Men who are older
Some vets
Some sick
Some young ones running from families that
threw them out after coming out.
Some from other countries
Others just finished a five- to ten-year bid.
Some twenty-somethings
working their way somewhere.

Lots of clothes that once belonged to someone else.

I keep not-sleeping.
Journal comes out.
I write to take it all in.
Maybe to escape.

Food distribution tomorrow on the parkway.
An interfaith effort led by a Masjid, Synagogue, Temple, and a
    Church,
the flyer by the bathroom says.

I trust.

reflections from the bottom

To be clear, I do not mean to bash our shelter system—either the shelters run by the city or those run by not-for-profit entities. These are essential safety nets that keep people alive. They are not beyond criticism. Like all institutions that are run by people, there can be difficult personalities working there. Those personalities can be amplified by low pay, difficult hours, and a near-perpetual busyness—let alone a population that isn't always easy to work with.

Yet, what does a critical take on shelters reveal? With system-looking eyes we focus not on the shortcomings of the band-aid. Rather we look at the cause of the wound in the first place. We don't ask what's wrong with the shelters; we ask what's wrong with the city that needs thousands of beds for shelters. Emergencies happen—fires, natural disasters, a terrifying abuse that causes one to run. Indeed sometimes the bottom falls out of one's life because of addictions or mental and physical crises. Yet, when folks are there long term, it betrays either a callousness or a lack of awareness on the part of the surrounding community. Tragedies happen, but the prayer is that we as a society can rally to get people back up.

The safety net that flies below the trapeze is not meant to be a long-term resting place when performers fall. It's meant to catch them, save their lives, and help them get back on their feet so that they may once again ascend back up.

mira

(Thanksgiving—Year One)

"Madness. A reflection of the Divine?"
I began to write while waiting in line for food.
I had miraculously
stumbled on an interfaith group that was handing out sandwiches
    and socks.

I saw madness there.
Have-nots waiting in line
for food handouts
in a land of plenty like our country
is the real madness here.

But I saw madness—I stood just a few feet away from madness
or was she
one of the few thinking clearly?

She too has left all, and yet she has traveled much further than I.
Perhaps beyond the point of no return.
She'd never want to return.

She was mumbling to herself.
Yet, not nervously
The look on her face was not an anxious one.
She wasn't replaying an old conversation.
Her manner presented an open invitation
and I accepted it
walking close enough to hear her words
yet not to disturb.

Her name I would later learn was Mira.

Mira spoke:
"Lord Jesus Christ, Son of God, have mercy on me a sinner.
Lord Jesus Christ, Son of God, have mercy on me a sinner,
Lord Jesus Christ..."

There was room near where she was sitting and eating because
she seemed "crazy" and smelled. Her shoes were off and
her hair, brown and red hair, blew wildly.

Eyes aflame she said, "I have a question for you."

"Me?" I whispered.

"Yes.
Are you running from or running to?"

Sometimes all it takes to start a revolution is a question.
Her question would be my second burning bush.

She would be the third.

The place where we were sitting was frequented by street people
which makes it a great spot to hand out food and socks.
There's a group of benches
between the old public library
and the large public fountain
Public common dialogical spaces
Also safe for resting.

Mira was sitting alone on one of the benches,
eating and talking to herself
Across from her were two men talking.

They passed the time laughing at her
when her mumbling would grow in intensity.
They looked at me as if I was crazy when I sat down next to her.

"Don't get burned man!" one laughingly warned.

Another of the three mockers waved me over,
before I could answer Mira.
He began to tell me,
as a type of warning I suppose,
all about Mira.

He relayed how he's known her for ten years
(he paused to soak in the fact that he'd been on the street
    himself for that long
—a tragedy and indictment on the rest of us).

He described how she is a nun,
or I suppose was a nun.
When she first came out to the streets
she shared of her desire for what she called "incarnational
    prayer."

She left her convent with a desire
to be with
those whom she felt called to pray for and love.
This, he thought, was crazy.

I walked back over to Mira.

"Lord Jesus Christ, Son of God, have mercy on me a sinner…"
she began again, forgetting her first question. Perhaps forgetting
    all questions.

reflections from the bottom

While in seminary I met my first spiritual director—a nun named Sister Mary Macrina. From her I first learned of the Jesus Prayer. It is beautifully written about in a book called *The Way of the Pilgrim*. This is the story of a wandering young sojourner who desires to fulfill the Apostle Paul's charge to "Pray without ceasing."[101] Along the way he meets individuals who each play a role in his spiritual deepening. While it is much more a part of the Orthodox Christian traditions, more and more Protestants and Catholics have come to appreciate the simple profundity of this little prayer and the spiritual exercise found in repeating it. And while I was not Orthodox, I decided to "try it out."

I spent hours and walked miles saying it again and again. Sometimes out loud, sometimes in my head. At times I was conscious of what I was praying; at other times it had become my breath—praying it with my brain turned off or turned elsewhere. Many would say this is the point. To integrate the prayer so deeply within that it becomes a prayer of the heart, allowing one to "pray without ceasing."

I began to notice some strange things happen. From time to time, as I would pray this ancient prayer, I would begin to smell a strong aroma of incense. A smell that I had only come across in churches. I found myself slowed down, peaceful, when this holy scent with no visible source would come upon me.

Likewise, my dream life had changed a bit. I marveled that I was praying in my dreams. The prayer was getting in, deep within. I found new grace and new mercy. Small flowers or birds would move me to tears. A squirrel that didn't run away in fear would inspire a wide smile upon my face. I found that I had a freedom in worship I had never felt before. During hymns I would raise my hands and sing loudly, joyously, without a care as to who heard. I laughed to myself that I was either getting holier or getting crazier!

I wondered in my journal, "Is prayer meant to draw us in or rather outward?" I think that the answer is both. Contemplative and activist. The way of the contemplative activist is a challenging and narrow path, though she or he who can keep this balance may be used by God in a mighty way indeed.

a theology of the bottom, like all true theologies, must have its ecclesiastical and contemplative counterparts. In other words, what might a theology of the bottom look like prayerfully? It's a life that is not only incarnationally on the bottom, but one that spiritually gets down to the bottom of our souls.

running

(December 1st—Year One)

Are you running from or running to?

Running?
The reality is my feet hurt so much that I'm just walking
And hardly that.

Are you running from or running to?

I'm running to Love.
Running from pain.
Running down.
Running out.

I sensed a call out,
to leave something behind.
(Perhaps you do as well.)
A call to seek a new depth, new intimacy, a new…something.
But I also know that I left something.

Why am I out here?
Running from the repetitive jail that is middle-class life?
Running to freedom?
Running from inactivity and complacency?
Running to a call? To God?

Why did Moses run?
More than the fear of punishment for killing an Egyptian soldier.
He fled Pharaoh
and he ran to A Well.

I thirst.
That's why I ran.
Thirst.
That's why you are contemplating running as well.

Scripture says:
"Come out from them!"[102]
I have a question for you as well:
What must you leave—come out from?
And what must you run to?

reflections from the bottom

It is difficult to not bring some level of introspection to theological work. Though theology is "God-talk" (*theo-logos*), it most certainly speaks to and of us.

And this is true for a theology of the bottom. It calls forth questions of the self. "How am I experiencing a kind of spiritual or existential homelessness?" "What aspect of life must I come down from?" "Is there a part of my journey that needs to be brought from the margins to the center?" "What is the bottom of my life?"

A part of the radical democratic call coming from the bottom demands full participation. Democracy invokes the counting of all voices, including yours. Thus, if an essential aspect of this theological project is bringing folks from the margins to the center, you must not sit this one out. Bring yourself, participate, and do the work of reconstruction inside yourself as well.

plague—order of anonymous beggars

(July 4th—Year Two)

Due North? The Constitution.
East? Christ Church.
South? Independence.
West? Liberty.

Patriotic tourists visiting this
Old City.
Some families road-tripped
Others took the subway
to complete what for many is a pilgrimage
to the cradle of liberty.

The reenactors don colonial clothing and hats
standing in the shade to survive the triple-digit heat.
Breaking character during water breaks and smoke breaks.

Local actors during the fall, winter and spring
some waiting for a breakthrough
many acting for thelove of it.
During the summer, they are Ben Franklin and Betsy Ross and
    George Washington and unnamed soldiers and citizens.

They see us panhandling in Old City
Park Rangers are kind, but we're
"unpleasant to tourists" so we're told to not loiter and are asked
    to keep it moving.

You ain't seen bad for business yet.

Every thirty minutes tour guides touch off from Independence
    Mall
and visit the more than thirty historical stops within walking
    distance.
And there are bus tours, and bike tours, and short films
colonial culinary experiences, and exhibits, and more,
all going strong until the fireworks after dark.

We go Paul and Silas style
two by two.
Two in each tour group for the remainder of the day.

"How do you do?
I am your most obedient servant Thomas and
I welcome you to Philadelphia.
I have the distinct pleasure of giving you,
my dear sirs and madams,
a tour this morning.
If you'll just follow me…"

We follow a pre-drawn path
he follows a pre-written script
And all along the way
moderately funny and carefully cautious
inoffensive anecdotes
are thrown in to keep the tour not only interesting but
    entertaining as well.

We hit Elfreth's Alley,
the oldest residential street in the nation.
Our watches say 11:11 a.m.
And we begin.

"Pardon me, but could you help out the homeless?"

we say with hands extended towards whoever is standing next to
us.

Some give
Some ignore
Some walk away and leave the tour
Some curse
Some call the police
Some pull children closer
Some yell
Some ask what's going on
Some join in

"You don't look homeless. What is this?"
And then we try to educate about the causes of homelessness
what keeps people on the street and in the system
and what folks can do about it.
And then we keep begging.
Never sharing our name or our reasons for being out there.

And we beg of all the patriotic tourists—
all over Old City.
Up north in the Constitution Center
While sitting in the ancient pews of Christ Church
While passing through Independence Hall
Walking by the Liberty Bell.
We kept asking and asking and talking and talking
Paul and Silas
praying without ceasing.

The tour guides were simply overwhelmed.

We eventually walked away
laughing about the reactions of the families

and thinking that our plague
was over with minimal effect
and minimal legal trouble.

But the plague was far from over.

Live feeds, online chatter began immediately online.
Many posts were critiques about "this stunt"
but there were also many who were fans.
So much so that some decided to do it again the next day
without our knowing
at tourist locations all around the country.
Some, we would later find out,
were pranks,
"the homeless begging challenge"...
but others did so bringing real answers when asked what this was
about.

And all who received money after begging
gave what they received to a local agency
which provides services for folks experiencing homelessness.

Within a few weeks
something called the
Order of Anonymous Beggars
formed online with individuals
writing and sharing their experiences.
These begging experiences were not limited to guided tour
groups.
Some brave souls spent time on the streets
begging and
"walking in solidarity and incarnationally
with those experiencing homelessness."
The website and the associated social media accounts took off

and the number of individuals involved around the country grew
    more every week.
And their sign?
Their logo?
The red and black fox and bird symbol
from the night of our first plague.

They came down to be with us.
Descending to us.
Dissenting with us.

It only takes a small spark to light an entire bush on fire.

The gatherings at the benches grew significantly after this.
The movement was growing.

reflections from the bottom

Twelfth-century philosopher and rabbi Moses ben Maimon (more widely known as Maimonides) writes beautifully about the different levels of giving in his *Mishneh Torah*. In the Tzdakah section, Maimonides explores what he sees as the eight levels of giving.[103]

The "lowest" (eighth) level is giving but doing so reluctantly or unwillingly. The seventh is giving willingly, but in a way that is inadequate. The next highest is giving in a way that is adequate, but only after being asked. The fifth level is giving in an adequate way before being asked to do so. The fourth level is giving to a third party that will then pass along the gift to a recipient the giver does not know. An example of this might be giving to charity without knowing the ultimate destination of the donation. The third highest level of giving entails the giver remaining anonymous while giving to a known recipient. The second highest form is when both the giver and the recipient are anonymous. And the highest form is giving anonymously in such a way that the unknown recipient is no longer dependent upon others (for example, providing a job for someone so that they may provide for themselves).

The element of anonymity, according to Maimonides, brings a purer motivation with the welfare of the recipient being the primary reason for the giving.

Is this ethical read applicable to serving—begging—on behalf of another? If the begging is not for oneself but for others and one is known and celebrated, this is a generous and kind act. Yet, if one serves, begs on behalf of another with no one aware of anyone's identity—well perhaps this is a higher level of… begging?

the burning bush

(December 15th—Year One)

Front Street. Just about the end of the line in my city.

Three hundred years ago,
trading ships landed on the shore that was once here at Front
    Street.
A colonial port.
Some brought coffee
others brought tobacco
and some brought human chattel.
Women and men from the West African coast
stolen and chained
packed into the lower decks of vessels
where they lay and slept in their own waste.
Those who didn't survive the journey—
thrown overboard into the Atlantic Ocean.
Those who did,
upon their arrival to the colonies
and later the young nation,
were sold into lives of enslavement, forced labor, abuse, and
    degradation.

It was from this very spot
many enslaved women and men
were presented, examined
sold.

Reading the sign, I felt a lucidness that I had not felt in some
    time.
As a young professor

I taught a course on the historical origins of poverty.
Slavery and its somewhat overlooked legacy
of course played a big part.

I stood at the historic marker
Felt led to take off my shoes and socks
unsure if it was for reverence
or for madness.

There is a statue of a Native American across the street.[104]
Another reminder of a nation's shame.
I step gently across the hard concrete
and sit at his feet.
Tired from my trail of tears.
I fall asleep.

As I slept I dreamt of my father and mother.
In the dream, they too were on the streets with me.
My daddy stood next to me wearing broken chains.
Mom wore moccasins, a bead necklace, and feathers.

"Wake up son. Wake up." They called to me.

And I did.

Rather I was woken up.
I noticed that I wasn't the only homeless person in the alley that
    night.
An old lady
with
two gray trash bags
hiding what was left of a life long gone.

She wore a dark blue hood

her back leaning up against the wall.
In theory to guard against being snuck up on.
I woke up and saw her because she was screaming.

Two punches to the head
Too many kicks to the stomach
Screams drowned out by the laughter of the boys who were
    almost men.

Disoriented, tired and hungry,
I ran over.

We must always run over.

I ran over.
Shocked faces turned to me.
A dropped bottle.
Through the smell of alcohol, I yell
"Stop it!"

They stop beating her. And just before running away—
Lighter fluid and a match.

Her screams were drowned out by the laughter of the boys who
    were almost men.

Flames spreading over her clothes
she crawled over to the river and
threw herself over the barrier
splashing down into a darkness that
silenced her calls for help and mercy...

reflections from the bottom

Spiritual directors, counselors, and therapists often remind clients that "it's all connected." A person's childhood, their adult relationships, their phobias, their interests, their dreams, their addictions—it's all connected.

Homelessness is not an isolated phenomenon in a society. In the Americas homelessness descends from slavery and other terrible ancestors like segregation, failing education systems, cruel immigration policies, genocidal displacement of Indigenous Nations, systemic sexism, homophobia, the war and prison industrial complexes, and more.

a theology of the bottom must see the interconnectedness of systems, both present and historical. Thus any effort to end or greatly reduce homelessness must address the devastation caused by the decisions, policies, hate, and violence of the past. We must be a constructive theology as well as a reconstructive one.

plague—death of the firstborn

(September 3rd—Year Two)

Few drugs lull a college radical to sleep
like an upper middle-class
salary, job, good school for their kids,
and suburban living.
The college socialist
turns trickle-down charitable giver
when protests and teach-ins
are traded in for PTA meetings
and travel soccer.

After Freddie was killed in my Baltimore[105]
the sedated suburbs just shook their heads
when the demonstrations (some called them riots)
were in North Baltimore.

S*** got real when them
n***** talked about coming to Roland Park.
F*** that!

Another question from the benches in front of the library.
"Professor—why have all our plagues been here in the city?
I'm from the suburbs. They need to see this more than folks down
    here do."

Seven miles to Lower Merion
home of the Black Mamba.
Eight miles to Haverford
Nine to Bryn Mawr
Ten to Villanova

Eleven to Radnor

We marched
No we flew.
Not like birds
but more like gnats or flies.
Many small bites.
None fatal
but painful enough to get your attention.

High-school kids walked out of school and joined us.
Two synagogues handed out food and water.

We walked silently for the first leg.
Then the talking began.
Then the yelling
with some folks peeling off.
This was meant to be a march.
It was a run.

Poor Desperation
Youthful Defiance
met with
suburban disconnect
and
white fragility

We marched
no we flew
not like birds
but like bombers
with zero plan
all over the place.

Boots on flower beds
Black and Brown gardeners'
confusion turned to anger turned to high fives

Each red octagon found words added:

Don't STOP Believin'
STOP Stepping over the homeless
STOP in the name of Love
STOP Greedy Soulless Capitalism
STOP Wasting Food
Can't STOP us

We marched
and flew

BAM!

until we heard a gunshot.

A kid was killed. One of us.
Not a homeless brother or sister though
One of the housed who anonymously came downtown and ran
    back out here with us.

"I thought he was a bum! I'm, I'm, I'm sorry.
But I thought he was just a bum trying to rob me."

Don't Stop Believin'.

reflections from the bottom

Many cities have begun having large end-of-year memorial services for those who die on the streets or in the shelter system that year. Death by homelessness is extraordinarily painful. Lonely. Unnoticed. Nineties rap group Lost Boyz said, some of us die with a name, "Some die nameless."[106] To die "nameless" and alone is among our greatest failures as a society. John and Jane Does are brought to morgues and then remembered through the fog of a tragic anonymity.

Coming to the bottom is reconciling with the presence of death down here. Not neglecting it. Not romanticizing life on the streets. But being present with and aware that to visit the bottom is to be in the proximity of a forgotten death.

There is a simple grace asked of those who come down. Learn names. And be family to those who would otherwise die alone.

go down

(December 15th—Year One)

Go down Moses.
Those of you that wish to be liberators
I say again, Go down.

The way to freedom
the way to freedom work
is not found in the professional ascent
the corporate ladder
the stairs of the academy
or higher and higher political office
It is down.

We are sometimes called to fly and climb
but these are prelude
days of preparation for when we are called to jump
and dive in.

With hands shaking
I ran over to the long metal bar
that's there to save people from falling in.
I felt both courage and fear.
Very human.

The water?
Surprisingly peaceful.
A large dark glass only disturbed by the last few ripples
expanding away from the late-night visitor that it saved from
    burning
but now threatened with drowning.

This is like much charity, is it not?

Over the last few months on the streets,
I had forgotten about my loathing and terror of rivers and oceans.
It all came back
like an evil chill causing now not just my hands,
but my whole body to shiver.

And then I fell in
unsure if it was on purpose or by mistake.
These are the best callings

There is no terror like being in open water not knowing how to
    swim.
Struggling to stand and climb out on ground that is not there.

It didn't take long for me to begin to sink.
No panic though.
It was as if the Living River Water washed away the fear that had
    possessed me for all of these years.
As I began my descent
my first thoughts dwelled upon the irony of this ending.

When I saw images of my father and mother
I noted to myself that it is true that your life really does flash
    before your eyes
when you are about to die.
I heard my father say again, "Imagine!"
and my mother say "Wake up!"
Was I really just moments from seeing them again?
Were they and the others that I have said goodbye to gathering at
    the gate?

I was still holding my breath, but I was going to let go soon.

I was dying.
Nothing else mattered.
I didn't think of my degrees
how much money I had made
my tenure
teaching awards
or my book
"a theology of the bottom"
which would now never be published.

I thought about what was just moments away.

I closed my eyes and cried tears quickly stolen by the river.
I gave thanks to God for giving me a chance to live.
"Thank you for this life.
I loved.
I was loved.
I learned and I taught.
I failed and I was forgiven.
Lord Jesus Christ, Son of God, have mercy on me a sinner."

I closed my eyes and as I was about to give up holding my breath
    my foot hit something.
A chain that extended out from the wall of the boardwalk.
I grabbed it and began to pull myself up
desperately but confidently.
Once I broke the surface I again heard the old lady's voice.
Stretching as far as I could I grabbed a hold of my homeless sister
    who was badly burned
but alive and pulled her to the chain.
We both climbed out and lay on the walkway.
Breathing heavy
but thankful to be alive.

reflections from the bottom

Just jump in. Or fall. Either is fine. We are down here drowning. Sometimes swimming, sometimes drowning.

In my previous book *Pond River Ocean Rain*, I found myself reflecting on drowning as a type of metaphor for what our life in God might be.[107] We—in a sense—die to self, seeking to be something like a cup of water poured into the ocean. Going back from whence we came.

If it is true, as so many saints have said over the years, that we find the face of Christ in the poor, then let us jump into poverty and be with Him.

not crazy

(December 15th—Year One)

Reemergence after baptism
We are new?
Or washed?
Or finally as we were made to be?

Wet and cold like a new birth
I stared at the one bright star that shined through the smog or
    clouds or
whatever was blocking the heavenly host from this city.
Coughing broke my daze and
rolling over I saw a sister take off what remained of a burnt
    sweatshirt
to reveal not only badly burned arms,
but a face that was far more youthful than I had first thought.
This was no old "bag lady."
It was Mira.
Crazy Mira from the benches in front of the library.

"Thank you. Thank you,"
she whispered in between coughs.

Blue lips and chattering teeth could form no words.
I could only nod my head.

Still not having looked and seen who I was, she continued to
    speak.
"Those guys have been terrorizing people on the streets for the
    last several months.
Someone needs to do something—

at least say something about this.
It's as if people on the street don't count."

She stopped when she saw my face.

"You seem different," I began.
"Not as, I hate using the word, but not as
crazy,"
I said calmly as if we both didn't almost die a few minutes ago.

She sat up giving little notice to the fairly serious burns on her
     arms.
Without looking at me she began a story that I will never forget.

"Several years ago,
I promised myself that the day I told another soul what I'm about
     to tell you
would be the day that I went back.
Back to the convent.
And I think—I hope—it's time.

I was a nun.
I like to think that I still am a nun.
I was born in a small town in Maine called Naples.
I grew up on a beautiful lake that
by day refreshes locals and visitors and
by night is guarded by singing loons.
It was beautiful and I imagined myself living there forever.
But I was encouraged to go to college,
So I went.
Things changed when I saw city life.
Know what I mean?"

I slowly nodded not knowing where she was going with this.

I started to shiver,
but I tried to hide it,
sensing important words approaching.
Not to mention that I really didn't have anywhere to go or any
    other clothing to change into.

"I saw people on the street for the first time.
Not just poor people.
There was poverty where I was
but people didn't sleep on the street.
They didn't rummage through garbage cans or dumpsters for
    food.
So I tried to help.
I held canned food drives at my school
I volunteered at a soup kitchen.
But I kept getting so frustrated by how it
seemed like no one around me cared.
It became too much for me.
I hated the world
didn't want to live in society anymore.

I had always been a pretty religious kid
so I dropped out of school
and entered the novitiate of a religious order.
After a year, I was a fully professed nun.
I thought that I could continue to serve,
while unplugging from the world that I was growing to loathe.

But I could never shake my sadness
at the lack of care the world had for people on the streets.

I prayed and I prayed for years.
I walked a desert full of silence from God
for all of my twenties and thirties.

And then finally, God spoke.
I had a dream and in the dream I was homeless.
I kept making signs that read 'Look at us!'
and just one person looked.
But that's all it took,
because that one person got a few others to look
and they got others
and they got even more to open their eyes.
And see.

I had that dream
the night going into Ash Wednesday
and I sat with it over the course of Lent.
Do you know what Lent is?
Never mind.
Anyway, when Lent was over I decided to ask
for a leave from the order
to 'visit my family who needed me.'
I wasn't lying!
I came to the streets.
It wasn't hard to leave as
I'd already made a vow of poverty.
The hard part was that many of the folks on the streets
recognized me because our order
had been working with homeless populations for many years."

"I'm sorry to interrupt, but two things,"
I jumped in.
"One, are you OK?
Your arms look very burned.
And two, you sound awfully coherent.
The other day at the benches
You seemed..."
I said with what must have been a somewhat suspicious look on

my face.

"I'm fine. On both accounts.
I pulled the mentally ill act
because I didn't think the guys on the street who I knew from my
   time in the order
would understand why I left.

While I was in college for those three semesters, I was a theater
   arts major.
That is probably the one thing I miss about college.
Being in acting class and studying theater.
Right before I dropped out to join the order,
I took a class on performance art.
Long story short, that's what I have been doing out here."

She paused to try to read my face before she concluded her long
   confession.

"I have been...performing insanity...because the world is insane.
It's absolutely mad.
We walk into work each day
earning money that we spend on cars, clothes, and coffee
while someone is dying of starvation.
Someone whom we pass every single day.
In one part of the world,
restaurants are throwing out unused and uneaten food every day.
And in another kids can't even get clean water.
Countries spend billions and billions of dollars on different ways
   to kill each other,
but hardly spend a dime thinking up new ways to help the least of
   us live.
And worst of all, the real madness is that we don't care.
I'm not crazy. I am acting.

I am performing insanity because...
we need some insane people to
mentally unplug from the norm
and think of some insane ideas
that will make this 'healthy system' benevolently ill.

When I saw you in front of the library
I recognized you
from your books.
I was wondering why you were out here.
Maybe it's for similar reasons as me...
Look, I'm leaving.
I'll be fine, don't you worry about me.
I'm going back to the order.
But you—go do something crazy.
You're a professor.
Go teach.
Teach folks on the street.
And make anyone who will listen
crazy enough to think that things can change."

And with that, the Voice from within the burning bush was
    quieted.

reflections from the bottom

That's it. It's a journey we all must go on. Each our own Exodus from our own Egypt. I mean this spiritually. I mean this literally. For homelessness of all types.

Or stay. No one has to go. But home awaits.

At the end of this story, the final thing that I can say about why we should serve through the paradigm of a theology of the bottom is because we have all had someone dive in and swim down to the bottom to help us back up. This has been the case time and time again in my life. I have hit rock bottom and almost drowned there. But I have been pulled back up. Thank God. May I, may we do the same.

reprise

In the months and minutes
leading up to the
plagues and the exodus
Twice a week we gathered.
I often thought of Mira and the madness she robed herself in.
"Is it so mad to dream of something different?
Or is the madness in the acceptance of this norm?"

And with that I began our first conversation on the benches
in front of the library
where I first met my mad nun.

Eventually the "bench classes" weren't just comprised of folks
    that lived on the streets
we learned along with college and high-school students
and parents
and friends
and allies.

We formed circles like Paulo Freire.[108]

And this story too now has come full circle.

It's a story of Madness.
Duke smiles from the other side,
"Remember, We Love ya madly!"[109]

This is a theology of the bottom.

always lowercase.

Here's my hope.
I hope you refuse the norms in regard to poverty and
    homelessness.
Offering critical refusals[110]
I pray you cry out as a dissenting voice.

And then I pray you come down.
Descend from the safety of whatever house is sheltering you
and be vulnerable with us down here.

This looks different for everyone.
If you dare ask,
God will make it clear.
Everyone has a burning bush moment.
Yet very few of us pause
remove our sandals
and look into the fire.

Fewer still listen to the call
coming from within the miracle.
And it is the rare individual who overcomes themselves
and actually answers it.

The desert journey from enkindled calling to liberating plagues
must be trod very carefully
while dancing freely

My feet have trod this path
burned from the sand
bloody from the stones.

Migrated from careless personal *ascent*
to careful anonymous *descent*.

I write this
in story
in song
in graffiti
in poem
in prayer

I write it in dust on the ground
Free
like liberated poetry
And I give it all away

that you may find the flame in your own life
and follow its call.

That you will go out under the humble veil of anonymity and
shake down the walls of whatever Egypt you're living in.
That you can help
people (and perhaps yourself) cross into freedom in small or big
    ways.
And dance by the sea.

Explicit.[111]

postlude

I shall never forget when, as a young graduate student, I first came upon the powerful text *The Silent Cry*[112] by Dorothee Soelle where in the introduction she writes:

> All living religions represent a unity of three elements that…we may call the institutional, the intellectual, and the mystical. The historical-institutional element addresses itself to mind and memory; in Christianity it is the "Petrine" dimension. The analytical-speculative element is aligned with reason and the apostle Paul. The third element, the intuitive-emotional one, directs itself to the will and the action of love. It represents the "Johannine" dimension. The representatives of all three elements tend to declare themselves to be absolute and to denigrate the others as marginal; however, without reciprocal relationships among the three elements, religion does not stay alive.

The late theologian was right. She was right about many things, but in this case she was correct in critiquing the declarations of the three branches as absolute and of having no need for the other two, or for those "outside" of the faith for that matter. Absolutes are sustained by controlling powers that seek to keep that which is within pure. Information, definition, and vision are cast from the top and they may trickle down to the bottom and outward to the margins. Never the reverse. Thus, those who are in power get to tell the stories, write the theology, judge what is holy.

It was the goal of this little book to try something different. Different at least for me, and different I pray for theology, for the church which I have been blessed to have lived within, and for society in general. I do not claim to be a prolific or even successful writer/scholar by any measurement, but that which I have written up to this point in my career could be described as having been written "from the top." It was literally written in either my university office or my suburban home. I tried to draw from a certain credentialed level of "expertise" as I wrote about poverty, theology, spirituality, or whatever the subject matter of that book or article was. I wrote from the absolute and from the top.

This project was meant to be written from a different place—the margins and the bottom. The phrase "a theology of the bottom" is one that I arrived at after much consideration. Originally, I considered "a theology of the streets" as that is exactly where this theology was written and where it is lived. I wrote much of this book in my journal while spending time on the streets of Philadelphia, Pennsylvania and Wilmington, Delaware. However, I kept returning to this word "bottom." Rather than streets, or poor, or marginalized, "the bottom" seemed to be most applicable to the mission.

The word "bottom" is meant to signify several notions. Firstly, it is meant to convey an effort towards producing a theology from the bottom rather than the top of the ecclesial and theological hierarchy (to be consistent with Soelle's paradigm above, I would add from the bottom mystically as well). a theology of the bottom owes much to the thought of individuals like Antonio Gramsci who wrote that "all men (and women) are intellectuals"[113] and Paulo Freire whose *Pedogogy of the Oppressed* pushed for a democratic education which believed that teachers should also be students and all students should be teachers rather than the model perpetuated by the hierarchical top-down "banking educational" system.[114] But do you see what I did right there? In justifying (clarifying) this theology I (first) drew from the works of two reputable scholars. Walking down the stairs to the ground floor is difficult sometimes.

But of course, in this case, it is not only those with letters after their names and professorships who can "do theology" and be a source for this theology/theopoetic. There are many brilliant theologians outside of the academy doing some of the most profound theological reflection. Further, it is not only those in positions of leadership that can produce a vision for the church. I have met and engaged with many individuals whose sober and clear eyes can see just where the church needs to go if they/we are to live in a way more faithful to Christ's witness and call. a theology of the bottom comes from the bottom — or rather those thought of as being on the bottom — right where Jesus was when He walked the earth.

This theology is not simply a critique of hierarchy, but it is also an acknowledgement of those who are often left out of the theological reflection and ecclesial worship/life. Matthew Works,[115] the noted speaker and artist who is briefly mentioned in the first plague, has testified to the painful experience of homeless women and men who are shamefully locked out of worship services on Sunday mornings and also kept out of sanctuaries all week.

Homeless people sleeping on the street right outside of churches.

Not allowed to sit or sleep on the pews inside.

a theology of the bottom is the voice of the church on the street — the church outside. The Rev. Dr. Debbie Little,[116] who is also referenced in this book, knew this when she founded Common Cathedral and Ecclesia Ministries in a public space in Boston. Her street church was a lived theology and ecclesiology of the bottom.

The bottom is not just comprised of the poor, but also of the untouchables, the excluded, the struggling, the wretched, and the rejected. During the writing of this book, I found teachers in brothers and sisters who were struggling with addictions, walking through life with criminal records, who were trying to navigate mental health challenges, as well as individuals who were sleeping on benches and in shelters. They live on what may seem like the bottom of society, but they too are doing deep theology—deep "God-talk."

Finally, a theology of the bottom is a theology on the ground— grounded and foundational. No building can stand without the foundation that is on the bottom. And the foundation of the Christian house is Christ. Thus, this is a theopoetic of Christ—Who while being the capstone is also the foundation. Perhaps the most painful distortion of Christ's good news has been the dangerous advent and remaining of the triumphant "Constantinian Christianity."[117] This bringing of Jesus from the bottom, on the cross as a homeless criminal, to the palace as a justifier of war and oppression is among the most cleverly diabolical ruinous acts to happen to Christianity and all people of faith.

Without question, people of great resources and power can be solid and loving people of faith. Grace and divine love are not limited to the poor. Yet, to warp the Jesus story (and in fact the faith narratives of nearly all religious leaders) so as to fit structures of power that wish to remain at the top is so far adrift from the Jesus of the Bible and the historical Jesus that Jesus Himself would hardly recognize His church were He to walk through much of our world today.

I suppose this is the gentle nudge that this book is trying to make. Maybe not so gentle. Come back down to the bottom! "Come out from them!"[118] And let's try Christianity—and the great faiths of the world—as they were originally meant to be practiced. Let's truly try to follow our Lord.

In these pages, the wisdom from the margins and the light from the bottom has been shared. This is not me. I am embarrassed that my name is on the front of this book. It's as inaccurate as a church or ministry bearing the name of the senior pastor on a sign in front (it's not their church, but rather God's). The pastor is simply the "under-shepherd," a vessel spoken through, representing something much bigger. The same is true here. I am representing something much bigger as well and I pray that the attention not focus on me, but rather those on whose behalf I write. I have no illusion of this text being more important than it is. But I do pray that it changes you, maybe changes your congregation, and maybe even your classes. At the very least, it has changed me.

When I first began this project, I shared part of it with two different friends and they both had the same suggestion: that while writing this, I needed to spend some real time on the streets. This was convicting (and this message is reflected in the exchange between the student and the professor when he is asked "How can someone write about the bottom when they have not been there?"). I had previously passed through the bottom, but I can't say that I had been there. I certainly had my share of "poor moments" during my economically up-and-down childhood and I certainly saw a lot when I did street outreach for an agency that served individuals experiencing homelessness in Philadelphia, but seeing something is very different than living something.

Thus, during days when my schedule permitted, I spent time "undercover" on the streets. I panhandled, I sat and slept on the street, I walked and walked and walked. Fully aware that this experience would be incomplete as I always had a home to go to at the end of the day, or after a long night there were always loving arms waiting for me, and that I had a bank account not too far away even if I had no cash in my pocket, I gained at least a little bit more of an understanding. I received the scornful judgmental looks thrown my way when I asked for money (which I donated at the end of each day). I deeply felt the rejection when people didn't want to touch me, or get too close to me, or wanted me to leave the coffee shop or store. I felt the hopelessness in humanity when hour after hour would go by without anyone sharing just a little bit of pocket change, a cup of coffee, a smile, or even a humanizing hello. I understood the temptation to talk to oneself when no one else will talk to you. Being on the street is complex. I felt so many feelings out there—pain, but also a freedom. I missed my wife and children, but that was about it. I didn't miss money, or technology, or the stress that my work so often brings. I could hear Francis, Gandhi, Dorothy Day, and many others from history whispering an invitation to stay.

Yet, I don't want to romanticize the experience of being on the street. It's terrible. It's unfair, unjust, and unloving that some of us must live (and survive) out there/down there.

Reality in writing is a complicated thing. And it is in this project. There is a lot in this story that is very true. Aaron and Ellie are/were real (and the story about the baby doll hustle is true). The three addicts under the bridge are based on a group of men I helped pick up when doing street outreach in Philly. But things like the plagues aren't real. Not yet!

One final word about this project: More than any other editorial decision, I wrestled with whether this book should be published anonymously or whether I should put my name on it. This decision weighed greatly on me. Anonymity and the humbling of oneself are integral to the story, especially the professor's journey. Adding my name to this project in many ways runs counter to the walk modeled by the professor and the Order of Anonymous Beggars. Further, as someone who trends more introverted, I feel far safer when robed in silence.

God is often found in the tension. Yet, tension and complexity are not easy places to navigate. I have been to the bottom. And not just in a passing sense. I've been poor. Yet, I am not that today. I live in the suburbs. My wife and I have great jobs that allow us to maintain a certain quality of life. The tension felt by the professor at the beginning of his journey is one that I have felt as well. "How can someone write about the bottom if they are not there?"

However, while holding this decision, the words "Your

playing small does not serve the world"[119] have been very present in my spirit.

So many of our decisions come down to questions of either fear or love. Keeping my name off was primarily driven by fears of looking like a hypocrite or a fear of unwanted attention. Fear is never a good motivator or compass for important decisions. Thus, I add my name in Love.

Writing this book has been a more profound experience personally than I had imagined. I came to the end of this project deeply moved. Once someone leaves and visits the bottom, they cannot return the same. I saw the face of Christ in the unhoused. How can I leave Him there? I am trying not to. I don't know what this will look like in the future, but I am beginning with one act. All of the royalties of this book will be given away.

Thank you for reading. May God bless you.

I write it in dust on the ground
Free
like liberated poetry
And I give it all away.

Chaz Howard

about the author

The Rev. Charles (Chaz) Lattimore Howard PhD is an Episcopal priest, theologian, and university chaplain at the University of Pennsylvania—his alma mater. Prior to his return to Penn, he served as a street outreach worker to individuals experiencing homelessness in Philadelphia, as well as both a hospital and hospice chaplain.

His writing has been featured in such publications as *The Philadelphia Inquirer*, *The Christian Century*, *Sojourners Magazine*, *Christianity Today's Leadership Journal*, *Chronicle of Higher Education*, *The Huffington Post*, *Black Theology: An International Journal*, *Daily Good*, *The Forward*, and *Slate*.

He is the editor of *The Souls of Poor Folk*, a text which explores new ways of considering homelessness and poverty, and the author of *The Awe and The Awful*, a poetry collection and Lenten devotional; *Black Theology as Mass Movement*, a call to theologians to expand the reach of their theological work; *Pond River Ocean Rain*, a collection of brief essays about going deeper with God; and *The Bottom: A Theopoetic of the Streets*, a Mosaic liberation theology novel-in-verse about the hero's journey downward to the street.

A son of Baltimore and a Godson of Philly, he shares life with his beloved wife, Dr. Lia C. Howard, and their three daughters. He sees his vocational calling to be to work for a communal increase in joy, peace, justice, and love.

note from the author

It means a lot to me that you have purchased a copy of this little book. All of the royalties will be given away to organizations that are working to address some of the challenges seen in this book. I do so hope that you have been as blessed in the reading as I was in the writing. If you have a few moments, please feel free to add a review of the book to your favorite online site. Also, if you would like to connect with other articles, essays, and books that I have written please visit my website http://www.charleslattimorehoward.com

With gratitude and hope,

Chaz

endnotes

1   The Gospel of Matthew 8:20.

2   T'Challa/Black Panther first appeared in Marvel Comics and was created by Stan Lee and Jack Kirby. Storm is also a character from Marvel Comics and was created by Len Wein and Dave Cockrum. Cyborg was created by Marv Wolfman and George Pérez and first appeared in DC Comics. These three early Black comic-book characters captured my imagination and inspired me as a kid. They still do.

3   Portions of this preface first appeared in "The Frederick Buchner Essay Contest" 2017, August piece "Power to the Imagination" that I wrote for *The Christian Century* (Volume 134, Number 17).

4   *Sfumato* is a term used primarily in artistic contexts to describe a painting technique most often attributed to Leonardo da Vinci. It alludes to the smoky blurring of borders between subjects in a work of art so as to create, perhaps ironically, a clearer and more realistic image for the viewer.

5   A theme powerfully explored in author Susan Howatch's Church of England book series (Fawcett Crest Books). Through her characters she plumbs the complex human experience of presenting a "Glittering Image" of ourselves for others to see while we hide the "Absolute Truth" of who we really are beneath.

6   A gentle and loving nod to *The Mirror of Simple Annihilated Souls and Those Who Only Remain in Will and Desire of Love* by the Beguine, Marguerite Porete.

7   Tupac Shakur, *Rose that Grew from Concrete* (MTV Books 2009).

8   I will always remain indebted to Dr. Stephen Ray. Stephen was an adviser of mine in graduate school and was a

member of my dissertation committee. His charge to me to do Black Liberation Theology vocationally no matter what job I had has stuck with me over the years. And it was from him that I first learned the term "reconstructing the center."

9   James Spady is, I believe, one of the great journalists and scholars of the twentieth and twenty-first centuries. Most of his articles were featured in Black-owned and run newspapers like *The Philadelphia New Observer*, though he's been published widely in academic journals around the world. And most of his books were self- or locally published. His brilliant, authentic, and free way of writing is something that I have sought to employ in my own work.

10   Benjamin Franklin is in many ways very much both the Enlightenment and the Age of Revolution personified. Wonderfully, he is also described as a Renaissance man.

11   Referring to the events that occurred during the Civil Rights Movement on March 7th, 1965 on the Edmund Pettus Bridge in Selma, Alabama.

12   Referring to the great non-violent leaders, demonstrators, prophets, Bayard Rustin and Mohandas Gandhi.

13   Referring to the painful yet crucial protest by children in Birmingham, Alabama in May of 1963 led by Rev. James Bevel.

14   Referring to the twenty-four-day Salt March or Dandi Satyagraha of 1930 in colonized India led by Mohandas Gandhi.

15   Referring to the inspiring student-led demonstrations in 1989 for democracy.

16   I use the name Mira in homage to both the dancing Miriam of the Exodus narrative in Torah and the dancing Mirabai of Hindu poetry.

17   A name for the place where Jesus Christ died.

18   Shabbat is the day of rest for many individuals within the Jewish tradition. Kabbalat Shabbat is the "welcoming of the

Sabbath," which includes certain readings, prayers, and a turning of the heart.

19 Jummah is the Friday prayer service observed by many Muslims. Jummah Mubarak is a greeting offering blessings on the one attending Jummah.

20 "Street Dreams" by Nasir Jones, Samuel Barnes, David Stewart, Annie Lennox from the album *It Was Written* (Columbia Records 1996).

21 "Thug Life" was the name of a group led by the late Tupac Shakur. That group also released an album by the same name, *Thug Life: Volume 1* (Amaru, Interscope, and Out Da Gutta Records 1994). The phrase "Thug Life" was also tatted across Pac's stomach. There is a lot to be said about the meaning of the phrase as a way of life, as an explanation for certain behaviors, and even as a tribute to Pac himself. One of Pac's interpretations of the THUG Life was, "The Hate You (U) Give Little Infants F***s Everyone." Angie Thomas applied the same definition in her moving bestselling book turned film, *The Hate You Give*.

22 I first heard this as a definition of Black Liberation Theology in conversation with the brilliant scholar and professor Stephen Ray.

23 It is difficult to write about the Bottom and the institutions that displaced it—not only because I have long been connected to one of those institutions (and indeed have great love for it), but because this is not my story to tell. I never lived in the Bottom—though I have known several dear friends who did. Suffice it to say, however, that what was once a community of families, dreams, and indeed struggle, has now been replaced by educational, research, and business buildings. This was not the only community knocked down by the gentrification of the twentieth century in Philadelphia. Other immigrant communities found themselves displaced as well.

24 These are among the great Hip Hop artists from the City of Brotherly Love and Sisterly Affection.

25 These words are found in the moving track "What We Do" by Philadelphia Freeway featuring Jay Z and Beanie Sigel.

26 An example of this is found in the brief but powerful unpublished autobiography of Nathan Mosel. The archives of the University of Pennsylvania have a copy.

27 Exegesis is the drawing out of a meaning. Explanation. The term is often associated with holy scriptures. A class or a Bible study might exegete a passage from the Bible in an effort to better understand it.

28 In America, activists in the late 1960s were saying "Power to the People." Activists of the same time-period in France were saying *"L'imagination au pouvoir."* "Power to the Imagination." This pointed towards the importance of art, the importance of imagining something new for our society.

29 The X-Men were created by Stan Lee and Jack Kirby for Marvel Comics. They are different than regular humans as they are mutants that are born with special abilities. One can see how their being born different and then being discriminated against because of those differences speaks to minority populations.

30 Lois Lane is a character in DC Comics and was created by Jerry Siegel and Joel Shuster. Her character is a journalist, sometimes hero, and long-time love interest/ wife of Superman. Mary Jane Watson in many ways is her counterpart in Marvel Comics, being the long-time love interest/wife (as well as actress and sometimes hero) of Spider-Man. She was created by Stan Lee and John Romita Sr.

31 Clark Kent/Superman was created by Jerry Siegel and Joel Shuster for DC Comics. Peter Parker/Spider-Man was created by Stan Lee and Steve Ditko.

32 The character Bruce Wayne/Batman was created by Bob

Kane and Bill Finger for DC Comics.

33   Trayvon Martin was a teenage African American man. I don't want to simply write about his death because he was certainly more than that. Yet, he became internationally known after his tragic death resulting from a racial profiling incident in Florida in 2012. In many ways, his death, the lack of judicial accountability, and the resulting activism helped to spark the spirit of the Black Lives Matter Movement.

34   "We Real Cool" is a poem written by Gwendolyn Brooks and first appeared in her collection of poetry *The Bean Eaters* (1960).

35   This quote is often attributed to Nelson Mandela but should actually be attributed to Marianne Williamson from her book *A Return to Love: Reflections on the Principles of "A Course in Miracles"* (HarperOne 1996).

36   The concept of the gaze speaks to how one's behavior can be influenced—sometimes in disingenuous ways—by the attention of other individuals from certain demographics. There are several factors to include in an explanation like this, but an example could be as simple as siblings acting and speaking a certain way when it's just them, but when a parent enters the room they change their behavior (so as not to get in trouble or be judged). This can be expanded to the impact of the White gaze on Black individuals, the male gaze on women, and several other scenarios. It is an audience that both affects the actors on stage and in a sense gives them the script.

37   Kirk Jones writes of the concept of moving through life at a "Savoring Pace" in his book *Addicted to Hurry: Spiritual Strategies for Slowing Down* (Judson Press 2003).

38   Dennis Rodman retired from the National Basketball Association as one of the best rebounders in league history. His nickname was The Worm.

39   Hebrews 13:2 (NIV) says, "Do not forget to show hospitality

to strangers, for by so doing some people have shown hospitality to angels without knowing it."

40 Siddhartha Gautama—the Buddha—gained enlightenment under the Bodhi Tree in Bihar, India.

41 In his must-read classic on education *Pedagogy of the Oppressed*, Paulo Freire writes about the importance of democratic education and the notion of all who are gathered in educational spaces being both teacher and student.

42 Referring to Jalal ad-Din Muhammad Rumi, the brilliant transcendent poet. Much of this effort is based on his writing and witness. Often, his work as a religious and community leader is missed because of the attention only given to his poetry.

43 Leonardo Boff is one of my favorite theologians and his work around articulating, teaching and then living Liberation Theology flows through this entire project.

44 This of course refers to Francis of Assisi—another whose radical work is lost in one facet of his life. He was so much more than a lover of nature. His revolutionary, Christ-like witness has meant so much to me.

45 Trench foot is a disease that results from prolonged exposure to wet, damp and cold conditions.

46 Philadelphia's Mural Arts Program led by the visionary Jane Golden has created stunning multi-story installations on the sides of buildings all around the city. They invite neighborhood residents to participate in many of their projects both in the design and production stages. Much has been written about the role that beauty plays in neighborhood restoration.

47 Mirabai is one of the world's great religious poets. While her devotional poetry was written from a Hindu perspective, it has a transcending courageous love that has spoken to me since I first read it.

48 This Fyodor Dostoevsky quote was a favorite of the radical

Catholic activist, writer, and leader Dorothy Day.

49 Emily Dickinson—the brilliant American poet—penned this phrase in her poem "Tell all the truth, but tell it slant."

50 I first met Matthew Works while I was a seminary student at Andover Newton Theological School outside of Boston. We would then connect again through Ecclesia Ministries. His moving and prophetic art is a favorite of mine.

51 The Gospel of Matthew 8:20.

52 Shane Claiborne wrote about this in an article he penned for *Sojourners Magazine* in 2018: "Why We Go to Jail: A Brief History of Christian Civil Disobedience."

53 This is a reference to the famous Malcolm X quote. It is often misunderstood and used to perpetuate the stereotype of violent and dangerous Black folk.

54 This is a reference to the quote by Frederick Nietzsche that I often return to: "He who fights with monsters might take care lest he thereby become a monster. And if you gaze for long into an abyss, the abyss gazes also into you." *Beyond Good and Evil* (1886).

55 Cornbread and Cool Earl were real individuals who in the early days of Hip Hop were popular graffiti artists. Graffiti is one of the pillars of Hip Hop. Whenever I teach my course on Hip Hop and Faith, the debate about whether graffiti is indeed art becomes a topic of debate.

56 See (or rather listen to) Childish Gambino's "This is America."

57 The role that the media plays in social activism is crucial, complex, and warrants more than just a footnote. Consider the relationship the organizers of the Birmingham Campaign during the Civil Rights Movement had with the news media. They certainly knew the way the country and the government would be moved by seeing images of people—including young people—being bitten by dogs and sprayed by fire hoses. The media's capturing of these

convicting images was essential in the turning of the tide of that movement. Further, the media helps to tell the stories that we are still talking about today.

58 American Congressman and Civil Rights activist John Lewis has been known over the years to encourage listeners to "get into trouble—good trouble!"

59 This is of course from the Rev. Dr. Martin Luther King Jr.'s famous "I Have a Dream" speech.

60 A version of this reflection first appeared as an article for Evangelicals for Social Action.

61 Students at Harvard University's Divinity School and College worked with local clergy to found the Harvard Square Homeless Shelter in response to the sharp increase in individuals sleeping on the street.

62 "Nessun Dorma" is a famous song from the opera *Turandot.* Perhaps the most famous person to sing it is the late but eternal Luciano Pavarotti.

63 Beat boxing has long been a part of music and specifically Hip Hop. Beat boxers use their mouths to simulate the sounds made by drums (or now drum machines). Few have done it like Dougie Fresh and Biz Markie. "Make the music with your mouth, Biz!"

64 See endnote 36.

65 "Cooning" is a term that uses an old derogatory name for African Americans ("Coon") to describe the act of being a Black person who is making a fool of themselves for the entertainment of white folks—particularly by playing up racial stereotypes in the "entertaining acts."

66 Gideon's Bibles have become famous not only for being in many hotel nightstand drawers, but also for being small in size, allowing for them to be distributed and carried around easily in one's pocket.

67 A definition of what Womanist Theology is also deserves far more than a few sentences in a footnote. Go research

it yourself! Yet, as an introductory statement if this is the first time you are hearing about it, Womanist Theology (or Womanist scholarship more broadly) speaks to Feminist efforts, yet specifically the efforts by women of African descent—as their experiences, while similar in some ways, are distinct from those of their white counterparts. The term "Womanist" draws from an Alice Walker phrase, "Womanish," featured in *In Search of Our Mothers' Gardens*.

68 Paulo Freire, *Pedagogy of the Oppressed*, 30th anniversary edition (Bloomsbury Academic 2014).

69 See Antonio Gramsci, *Selections from the Prison Notebooks* (International Publishers Co. 1989, reprint).

70 Again from "What We Do" by Freeway.

71 "Shuckin' and jivin'" is an old slang term among many Black folks connoting "messing around." Playing around while doing work.

72 Again from "What We Do" by Freeway.

73 HALT is an old Alcoholics Anonymous (AA) acronym standing for Hungry, Angry, Lonely, Tired. In those moments in life when we are hungry, angry, lonely, or tired we are especially vulnerable to following our addictions/relapsing—and we should be on guard. Bill W. is the founder of Alcoholics Anonymous. AA has been a blessing in my life.

74 *The Trinity*, also known as *The Hospitality of Abraham*, is a famous fifteenth-century icon by Andrei Rublev.

75 This, like much of this book, is based on a true story. A version of this happened while I was working in street outreach for Project HOME.

76 From "Lift Every Voice and Sing" by James Weldon Johnson and John Rosamond Johnson (1900 and 1905).

77 *I Wonder as I Wander* is the name of the autobiography by the great Langston Hughes.

78 Within some religious communities, especially within certain

Jewish traditions, the name of God is so sacred that it should not be uttered or even written. Thus, some individuals refer to the divine name as Ha-Shem or simply The Name.

79   Theater of the Oppressed is a theatrical form first developed by Augusto Boal in Brazil.

80   There is an improvisation game called "Yes and…" where actors/players tell or act out a story incorporating what the previous speaker introduced. An example could be, "I am a farmer working on my crops." "Yes, and…I am growing magic beans!" "Yes, and…these beans will give you super-strength if you eat them, *yum yum*." "Yes, and I will use that strength to fly around the world to work to alleviate hunger." And so on.

81   President Ronald Reagan's administrations (first as Governor of California and then as President of the United States) took actions and passed policies that greater hurt unhoused individuals wrestling with mental health challenges. In California, he signed the Lanterman–Petris–Short Act, which closed most state-run mental health institutions and replaced them with outpatient facilities. There were certainly issues with many of the institutions, yet without the support they were receiving inside, many individuals who could not live independently (and didn't/couldn't live with family members or friends) were then on the street, and remain there. As president, he and his administration gutted funding for mental health patients, having a similar effect.

82   "War of the Roses" by Janelle Monáe, featured on her album *The ArchAndroid* (Wonderland/Bad Boy 2010).

83   From "Immigrant" by Sade, featured on her *Lovers Rock* album (Epic 2000).

84   There are many cities in the US with cruel laws that oddly fine people money…for asking for money. And when they can't pay the fines they are locked up. Something we can do

is work to change unjust and unhelpful laws like these.

85   These last written words of Martin Luther's were found at his desk written half in German and half in Latin.

86   I wish I had more to cite here. Anne Marie was a joyous and brilliant friend. Praying she is blessed wherever she is!

87   The Rev. Debbie Little, an Episcopal priest—indeed a street priest. She founded Common Cathedral, which was an outdoor street church that grew into Ecclesia Ministries.

88   The Welcome Church is a phenomenal organization that gathers for worship, but also supports unhoused individuals in many other beautiful ways.

89   The planners for the City of Philadelphia worked hard to include public spaces—commons—where different individuals from a range of backgrounds could share space and be in conversation with one another. One such space or square in Philly is Rittenhouse Square.

90   Psalm 133:1.

91   This quote has been used as a compass by activists and individuals in the prophetic stream ever since.

92   Philadelphia is one of two cities that claim Billie Holiday— the other being Baltimore.

93   "Strange Fruit" by Abel Meeropol in 1937. It would later be performed and recorded by Billie Holiday.

94   "In Da Club" by 50 Cent, featured on the album *Get Rich or Die Tryin'* (Aftermath/Shady/Interscope/Universal 2003).

95   In an interview in a parking lot, when asked about whether he had written a check to pay a fine yet, the NFL great Randy Moss replied that when you're rich you don't pay checks. When asked then how he paid, he replied by saying, "Straight cash, homie."

96   According to the Williams Institute, 40% of the homeless youth served by agencies identified as LGBT, 43% of clients served by drop-in centers identified as LGBT, 30% of street outreach clients identified as LGBT, and 30% of clients

utilizing housing programs identified as LGBT. This is an underdiscussed aspect of homelessness.

97 Ephesians 6:12.

98 "Out Beyond Ideas" by Rumi.

99 2 Corinthians 3:17.

100 "Elastic Heart" by Sia, featured on her album *1000 Forms of Fear* (RAC 2015).

101 1 Thessalonians 5:16–18.

102 2 Corinthians 6:17.

103 The great Jewish rabbi, scholar, and philosopher Maimonides (Rabbi Moshe ben Maimon) wrote about eight levels of charitable giving in his *Mishneh Torah*.

104 In Old City, Philadelphia, there is a statue portraying Chief Tamanend of the Lenni-Lenape Nation. The statue is facing the statue of William Penn which sits atop of City Hall some fifteen blocks away. Tamanend was one of the most celebrated individuals in the American colonies and early years of the young nation. He was celebrated because of his willingness to work with, partner with, trade with, and coexist with the early Europeans who came to Pennsylvania. Thus, statues, clubs, and even holidays were erected, founded, and established in his honor. It is important to note that there is so much more to the story of the relationship between Native Americans and Europeans. And much if not most of that story is tragic and cruel.

105 Freddie Gray died in 2015 from injuries sustained during a "rough ride" (an intentionally bumpy ride in a police wagon while individuals are restrained by handcuffs and ankle restraints, disallowing them from protecting themselves from being thrown around the back of the van during harsh turns). His death at the hands of police officers enraged my fellow Baltimoreans, resulting in one of the many landmarks of the Black Lives Matter Movement.

106 "Lifestyles of the Rich and Shameless" by Lost Boyz,

featured on their album *Legal Drug Money* (Uptown/MCA 1995).

107 My last book was *Pond River Ocean Rain* published by Abingdon Press in 2017. It's a very different feel from this book, but in many ways pours into the spirit of what I've tried to articulate here.

108 In his must-read classic on education *Pedagogy of the Oppressed*, Paulo Freire writes about the importance of democratic education and the notion of all who are gathered in educational spaces being both teacher and student.

109 Duke Ellington ended many of his shows with this phrase.

110 A phrase made famous by the radical philosopher Herbert Marcuse.

111 A gentle and loving nod to *The Mirror of Simple Annihilated Souls and Those Who Only Remain in Will and Desire of Love* by the Beguine, Marguerite Porete.

112 Dorothee Soelle, *The Silent Cry: Mysticism and Resistance* (Fortress Press 2001).

113 Antonio Gramsci, *Selections from the Prison Notebooks* (International Publishers Co. 1989, reprint).

114 Paulo Freire, *Pedagogy of the Oppressed*, 30th anniversary edition (Bloomsbury Academic 2014).

115 Matthew Works is a formerly homeless artist who has held exhibits and lectured in galleries and universities around the US.

116 See endnote 87.

117 The best articulation of this, I believe, was made by Cornel West in *Democracy Matters: Winning the Fight Against Imperialism* (Penguin Books 2005).

118 2 Corinthians 6:17 (NIV), "Come out from them and be separate, says the Lord."

119 Again from Marianne Williamson from her book *A Return to Love: Reflections on the Principles of "A Course in Miracles"* (HarperOne 1996).

TRANSFORMATION

Recent bestsellers from Changemakers Books are:

Integration
The Power of Being Co-Active in Work and Life
Ann Betz, Karen Kimsey-House
Integration examines how we came to be polarized in our dealing
with self and other, and what we can do to move from an either/
or state to a more effective and fulfilling way of being.
Paperback: 978-1-78279-865-1 ebook: 978-1-78279-866-8

Bleating Hearts
The Hidden World of Animal Suffering
Mark Hawthorne
An investigation of how animals are exploited for
entertainment, apparel, research, military weapons, sport, art,
religion, food, and more.
Paperback: 978-1-78099-851-0 ebook: 978-1-78099-850-3

Lead Yourself First!
Indispensable Lessons in Business and in Life
Michelle Ray
Are you ready to become the leader of your own life? Apply
simple, powerful strategies to take charge of yourself, your
career, your destiny.
Paperback: 978-1-78279-703-6 ebook: 978-1-78279-702-9

Burnout to Brilliance
Strategies for Sustainable Success
Jayne Morris
Routinely running on reserves? This book helps you transform
your life from burnout to brilliance with strategies for sustainable
success.
Paperback: 978-1-78279-439-4 ebook: 978-1-78279-438-7

Goddess Calling
Inspirational Messages & Meditations of Sacred Feminine
Liberation Thealogy
Rev. Dr. Karen Tate
A book of messages and meditations using Goddess archetypes
and mythologies, aimed at educating and inspiring those with
the desire to incorporate a feminine face of God into their
spirituality.
Paperback: 978-1-78279-442-4 ebook: 978-1-78279-441-7

The Master Communicator's Handbook
Teresa Erickson, Tim Ward
Discover how to have the most communicative impact in this
guide by professional communicators with over 30 years of
experience advising leaders of global organizations.
Paperback: 978-1-78535-153-2 ebook: 978-1-78535-154-9

Meditation in the Wild
Buddhism's Origin in the Heart of Nature
Charles S. Fisher Ph.D.
A history of Raw Nature as the Buddha's first teacher, inspiring
some followers to retreat there in search of truth.
Paperback: 978-1-78099-692-9 ebook: 978-1-78099-691-2

Ripening Time
Inside Stories for Aging with Grace
Sherry Ruth Anderson
Ripening Time gives us an indispensable guidebook for growing
into the deep places of wisdom as we age.
Paperback: 978-1-78099-963-0 ebook: 978-1-78099-962-3

Striking at the Roots
A Practical Guide to Animal Activism
Mark Hawthorne
A manual for successful animal activism from an author with
first-hand experience speaking out on behalf of animals.
Paperback: 978-1-84694-091-0 ebook: 978-1-84694-653-0

Readers of ebooks can buy or view any of these bestsellers by
clicking on the live link in the title. Most titles are published
in paperback and as an ebook. Paperbacks are available in
traditional bookshops. Both print and ebook formats are available
online.

Find more titles and sign up to our readers' newsletter at
http://www.johnhuntpublishing.com/transformation
Follow us on Facebook at
https://www.facebook.com/Changemakersbooks